Just Write!

**An Essential Guide for
Launching Your Writing Career**

Susan Titus Osborn

**WRITE
NOW!**

Write Now Publications
Phoenix, Arizona 85013

Published by Write Now Publications
A royalty division of ACW Press
5501 N. 7th Ave., #502
Phoenix, Arizona 85013
1-800-931-2665
www.acwpress.com

Printed in the United States of America by Bethany Press International, Bloomington, Minnesota 55438

ISBN 1-892525-25-9

This book is dedicated to the authors who mentored me, to the writers I have been able to mentor, and to my husband Dick for his wholehearted support.

Contents

Foreword
by Bob Hostetler

The form of a white-whiskered man hunched in the doorway. The stooped figure belonged to John, the fisherman who had once sailed the Sea of Galilee and walked the roads of Judea with Jesus of Nazareth.

But those days were long ago, thought the aged disciple, *and I am an old man.* Yet John still called Jesus "Master."

As John sat in the doorway of his home in Ephesus, a breeze from the harbor disturbed the papyrus sheet which was spread across his lap. John stared at the blank surface on his knees, as he had for many days now, not knowing where to start. There was so much to say. He had so many memories of the Lord; but when he tried to record them all, he froze with the scope of it all.

His mind flashed with the memory of the arguments he'd had recently with the young disciple who shared his home.

John argued, "Did not Matthew, John Mark, and Luke already record such things? What need is there of another Gospel?"

"But," the young man said repeatedly, "you yourself have told me many things they did not record."

Then the old man smiled and said, with the perspective of a lifetime, "Yes, but Jesus did so many things. If they were all written, I suppose that even the world itself could not contain the books."

"But," the other countered, with flaming eyes, "Matthew and the others were not confronted with the Gnostics as we have been! They did not deal with the lies these people are spreading."

The Gnostics. John quieted when they were mentioned. He knew too well the harm they had done in the young church with their teachings. *They were not there,* he thought. *If they had known Jesus, if they had seen Him, they would not imagine that Jesus was some ghostly presence inhabiting a human body. They can only deny the reality of His death with their mental gymnastics because they did not see it as I did. They weren't there when His mangled body came off the cross. I was there. I saw!*

He stood suddenly, dumping the papyrus from his lap to the ground. His joints creaked with age, and he winced from the pain. He thought of how it would have grieved Mary, whom John had cared for those last years of her life, to see her Son's Gospel polluted by such teachings.

The young disciple was right, of course. Another Gospel must be written. The Gnostics must be answered.

He sat again and picked up the sheet off the floor. *What do I write?* he asked himself. *How do I begin?* Jesus' aging friend looked silently across the harbor waters to the coral sunset of the western sky. Half a century had passed since Jesus had turned John's world—everyone's world—upside down. Perhaps it had been too long.

"My memory isn't what it used to be," he said aloud. Suddenly he was overwhelmed with the weariness of a lifetime and the blank surface of the page. He shook his head. "Perhaps if I were not so...so tired and writing were not so hard. There will be others. Younger men. They will write."

That scene, of course, is mostly out of my imagination. But what if John had not written? What if the aging apostle had left the writing to others? If John had not written, would the Gnostics have gained converts? If he had not written, would those who maintained the full truth of the Incarnation have been branded as heretics? If he had not written, would the true Church still be striving against a more powerful, accepted falsehood?

Of course, it's impossible to say, just as it would be impossible to say what might have happened had Augustine never written—or Martin Luther or John Calvin. Just as it's impossible to say what will happen if *you* don't write. It's impossible to say what child, young person, or adult might be affected if people whom God has gifted and called to write do not. In fact, part of the wonderful and providential ministry of this book, which you hold in your hands, is its ability to open to you an effectual door of ministry through the written word, to make it possible for you to participate in the exquisite privilege of writing…and of being published…and of being read.

I am profoundly grateful that I need not wonder how things might have been different if Susan Titus Osborn had not responded to God's gift and call to her. I shudder to think how Christian publishing—and how I as a Christian writer—would have lacked the enrichment and enhancement that Susan has provided over the years through her many excellent books and articles, through her years of editing *The Christian Communicator* and her ministry as director of the Christian Communicator Manuscript Critique Service, through her teaching at over 120 writers' conferences across the United States and in five foreign countries.

This book is but the latest installment in Susan's ministry of writing and teaching others to write. It is truly an essential guide to launching a writing career and an invaluable addition to any writer's library. Through the carefully crafted words of these pages, let her be your writing mentor, as she has so often done so well for so many.

Bob Hostetler is a Gold Medallion award-winning author who co-authors with Josh McDowell.

Introduction

When I began writing in 1978, a friend introduced me to Karen Wojahn, an author who agreed to mentor me if I, in turn, would promise to mentor others. She started me on the road to a full-time writing, editing, and teaching ministry.

If you are like I was, you may be wondering where to begin, how to polish your manuscripts, and how to explore the markets to sell what you write. This book will give you tips on getting your creative juices flowing, finding ideas and researching them, and learning to set aside time to write. It will cover the mechanics of grammar, punctuation, and word usage, as well as advise you of pitfalls to avoid. Article writing, short stories, devotionals, and writing for children are some of the specialty areas I cover. When you finish, you will have all the information you need to submit a professional-looking manuscript to an editor.

I have spent the past twenty-one years polishing my writing skills. Learning never ends. Now I'd like to pass the knowledge I've gained on to others. I have taught at more than 120 writers' conferences across the nation as well as in five third-world countries. I've also taught writing courses as an adjunct professor at three college campuses. For eight years, I was editor of *The Christian Communicator*. Today I continue to write a monthly column for that magazine.

Although I have written eighteen books, I don't think of myself as a great author. I am, however, a great encourager—and I love to teach. Today I direct the Christian Communicator Manuscript Critique Service. My staff and I critique between 200 and 300 manuscripts each year. We are thrilled when we receive a note from someone who has been critiqued by our service and has published his or her article or book.

The legacy I want to leave behind on this earth is skilled authors who will find a way to make Jesus Christ real for their readers. May this book be a tool in accomplishing that purpose.

Chapter One

Where Do You Begin?

Beneath the rule of men entirely great,
The pen is mightier than the sword.

—Edward Bulwer-Lytton, *Richelieu*

Perhaps you have a desire to write, to get published, and to glorify God; but you don't know where to begin. This book offers what you need to know to present to a publishing house a professional looking manuscript for an article or story. You will learn where to begin, how to begin, and where to go from there.

Thomas Alva Edison wrote, "Genius is one per cent inspiration and ninety-nine per cent perspiration." I agree that inspiration is only one percent of the job. Organization, tenacity, and execution comprise the other ninety-nine percent. In other words, writing is mostly hard work. I believe anyone can become a professional freelance writer if he or she has the desire and the perseverance to do it.

Writing perfects your craft like a musician perfects his tone on a cello. My son started playing the cello when he was in third grade. It squeaked terribly at first, but it wasn't long before he made beautiful music. When he was in high school, he gave up the cello for a couple of years and played keyboards. When he picked up his cello again, it squeaked. His playing had become rusty. Writing skills also become rusty from lack of use, so writers need to practice daily.

Writing Goals

Writers need to know their main purpose for writing. They may have a desire to share their stories with others. Perhaps they seek personal growth. For many Christians, writing is a ministry. Statistically only one percent of Christian writers make a living at their vocation. Personally, my main writing goal is to change lives and to share thoughts with others that will benefit them.

It might help you to set up a goal sheet and answer the following five questions:

1. What is your overall purpose in writing?
2. What are some actions you can take that will help you make writing a priority?
3. How much time are you willing to commit to writing each day to achieve your writing objectives?
4. What are your realistic writing goals for the next year?
5. What are your writing goals for the next five years?

As well as establishing goals for writing, you will need to decide what time commitment you are willing to make. Be aware that you can't wait until everything else is completed. Writing must become a priority. Other things may have to be sacrificed. If you aren't currently writing, you'll need to give up something you are doing now in order to gain the hours you plan to devote to writing. Make a commitment to set aside a definite amount of time to perfect your craft.

Now let's turn our attention to the writing process.

The Three-Step Writing Method

First Step: Theme and Outline

Before you begin to write your article or story, decide what your primary purpose is. The first step in the writing process is to state your theme in one word. Then state it in one sentence. Do this for short pieces and devotionals, for stories and articles, as well as for books. Each point must support the main theme.

Another way to look at this step is to say that your article or story must have focus. Focus is deciding on a general theme or premise and developing it throughout the piece. Most articles are rejected because the writer deviates from the premise or tries to tell too many stories in one article. One idea, well developed and remembered by the reader, is worth more than many thoughts read and forgotten.

Next, create a preliminary outline before you write one word of the actual manuscript. Set up headings for the points you want to cover in your article and subheadings if you think of them. This outline is only for your use, so it doesn't have to be fancy or follow exact rules.

After your outline is written, finish the first stage of writing your article, which is to develop your idea into a full page. Accomplish this task by using the analytical, or critical, side of your brain. First, get your ideas down on paper. Writing style shouldn't be a concern at this point.

An alternative to creating an outline is to use the "Wheel Method." Draw a circle in the middle of a page and write your theme in the center. Draw spokes emanating from the circle, and write concise thoughts about your theme. Do this in any order that thoughts come. After formulating as many ideas about your main theme as you can, arrange them in logical order to form an outline.

Second Step: Rough Draft

After finishing your outline, wait a few days before you begin the second step of the writing process, which is to write the first rough draft of your article or story. As you begin, let the theme and supporting ideas form in your mind.

Now, write your story. Turn off the critical side of your brain, and turn on the creative side. Let the words flow onto the paper. Don't get hung up on spelling, punctuation, or phraseology; just write whatever comes to your mind. Try not to think about your outline or theme sentence. Write the first draft in one sitting, picking a location and time to write that will allow for a minimum of interruption.

Get down on paper everything you can think of regarding your subject. You may end up with enough material for several articles. Don't worry about that, however, when you are writing this first draft. Or you may not have enough material. If you're short of words, you'll need to go back and add more information during the editing stage.

Third Step: Rewriting

Writing the first draft is the creative part. For me, this is the fun part. The hard part is rewriting, rewriting, and rewriting. What separates those who become published writers from those who would like to have written is a willingness to work through this process of polishing their work step by step. Polishing is always hard work, but the shine that results is worth the effort.

Your first stories, articles, or books may take a long time, but you will learn from practice. Even if it takes one hundred hours to write your first article, it is not wasted time. You will learn valuable lessons to apply to future writing, which will most likely flow smoother.

After you have written your first draft, set it aside for at least a week. It is easy to become so enthusiastic about your first draft that you are convinced it is ready for publication. Chances are, however, it is not.

James Michener wrote, "I have never thought of myself as a good writer. Anyone who wants reassurance of that should read one of my first drafts. But I'm one of the world's great rewriters."

When you pick up your manuscript for the third time, you've put some distance between your emotions and your work. Now you are ready to begin the *third step* of the writing process—editing your own work. You should be able to look at it more objectively. You can treat it like a jigsaw puzzle, rearranging some of the pieces to fit better.

First read through your first draft for an overview. Make a mark in the margin where it doesn't flow smoothly. Read quickly. Don't stop and ponder what is wrong. That will come later when you do the line-by-line editing.

Then go back and look at your outline and theme sentence. Do they need revision? Does your article or story support your outline and theme? If not, you need to change either your theme and outline or your first rough draft. Remember, *nothing* is set in concrete at this stage.

Ask yourself these twelve evaluation questions:

1. Do I have a good beginning?
2. Is my story or article interesting?
3. Is it significant?
4. Is my story or article marketable?

5. Does it have continuity?
6. Does it make sense?
7. Have I left out any important points?
8. Did I say what I wanted to say?
9. Do my paragraphs flow smoothly?
10. Did I repeat my thoughts?
11. Did I use complete sentences?
12. Does my ending tie into my beginning?

Now look at the opening sentence and paragraph. Do you hook the reader with your opening? Does it make the reader want to continue reading? Beginnings, for me, are the most difficult part of a manuscript to write. Often I end up throwing out the first three paragraphs or even the first page. Don't struggle too long on your beginning at this point. You can always come back and edit it on subsequent drafts. Or you may prefer to start with the middle and go back to write the beginning later.

The next step is to go carefully through your article, looking for spelling errors, missing punctuation, and incorrect grammar usage. Tighten your writing by eliminating unnecessary words. Rearrange the paragraphs and sentences to make your writing flow smoothly. Become familiar with such books as *The Elements of Style* by William Strunk, Jr. and E. B. White (New York: Macmillan, 1979) in order to learn the mechanics of grammar, punctuation, and word usage.

An excellent summary from Strunk and White is: "Vigorous writing is concise. A sentence should contain no unnecessary word, a paragraph no unnecessary sentences, for the same reason that a drawing should have no unnecessary lines and a machine no unnecessary parts" (p. xiv).

Chapter Two

Getting Your Creative Juices Flowing

*Lord, today, take this pen in your hand, and write your words of
love. Use me, Lord; make me yield to your guidance from above.
Make me your instrument, dear Lord, the pen within your hand.
That I may know what it means, to write your words to every man.*

—Van Trapp

In order to get your creative juices flowing, you will need to
increase your perceptivity to the world and the people around
you. Here are seven ways to accomplish this objective.

Develop Insatiable Curiosity

Those who have raised kids know that young children are
curious. Often the most popular word in their vocabulary is
"Why?" They explore their world by having their questions

answered by adults and their peers. As a result, their inquiring minds are constantly growing and learning.

In a similar manner, we adults need to develop insatiable curiosity. We need to find out how things are made and question why they are the way they are. We can find our answers by thoroughly researching the subject in books, by searching the Internet, and by talking to others. Don't be afraid to ask an authority in a field the answers to the questions you need for your research. Experts enjoy talking about their specific areas.

Learn New Skills

Our world is constantly growing and changing; and to stay abreast of it, we need to grow too. A good example is computer technology. Computer software and hardware have improved incredibly in the past five years. Learning how to edit on screen, cut and paste, and use the World Wide Web so you will have vast amounts of research information at your fingertips are time-saving skills to develop.

Another useful ability is to learn a foreign language. I live in Southern California where Caucasians are fast becoming a minority. My husband and I are learning Spanish together, which will be advantageous when talking to store owners, customers, gardeners, and others who cannot understand English well.

Learn to Take Risks

I'm not suggesting you place your life in danger but that you step out of your comfort zone and take some risks. Perhaps you could volunteer time at your local rescue mission or a home for unwed mothers. I have a friend who spends every Thanksgiving at a rescue mission with her family, serving turkey dinners. Her children have learned the true meaning of Thanksgiving by sacrificing their family time to help the less fortunate on this special day.

Visit New Places

I recently visited a remote village hospital in the Himalayan Mountains. The only way to get there was in a four-wheel drive vehicle over bumpy, windy roads with lots of hairpin curves and steep ledges. It was a long, cold, difficult journey; but the experience of seeing one doctor's commitment to the village people of that area was well worth my temporary discomfort.

You could take a new route to a place you often go. When I drive the extensive freeway system in Southern California, I don't find much fodder for my books. Sometimes I take a little extra time to drive down the Pacific Coast Highway which skirts the ocean all the way down to San Diego and up to San Francisco. My creativity is piqued by all I see. On an early morning trip, I once saw a huge pelican stretching and yawning in the morning sun. He had the biggest mouth I have ever seen. Several writing ideas popped into my mind immediately.

Open Your Mind to New Ideas

When I taught Christian writing in India, a number of Hindu students were in my class. I had studied Hinduism, and I made them feel welcome by referring to tenets of their religion. I made it clear, though, that I was running a Christian conference sponsored by a Christian organization. I was open to knowing about their faith without compromising my own in any way. It actually gave me the chance to witness through my teaching and life experiences.

Be Aware of All Your Senses

As you write, use all your senses so the reader can live the experience with you. Readers usually have vivid imaginations—that is why they like to read.

If you are describing the process of making buttermilk biscuits, you could start by listing the ingredients. Suggest using cider vinegar and milk if the cook doesn't have buttermilk on hand. Help the reader to picture the warm, inviting kitchen and feel the dough as she mixes the ingredients. Have her breathe in the smell of the biscuits as they cook in the oven. The anticipation of taking them out of the oven, breaking them open, and smearing them with butter and jam will make the reader's taste buds water.

Write from the Heart

We can use a similar emotional response within ourselves to evoke reactions in our readers. If we don't feel an emotion, we can't arouse that sensation in a reader.

Before you start writing, ask yourself, "What emotion do I want to evoke—compassion, anger, sadness, pain, fear, love, joy?" What arouses your passions? What do you care about? What do you want to change? How can you help others? In your writing, you need to have something to share that will benefit others, change their lives.

We don't have to undergo an exact experience in order to write about it, but we need to feel passionately about our subject. *You Start with One* is a book I wrote about a ministry in Sri Lanka that feeds and vocationally trains thousands of children a day. Because of the unrest there, I wasn't able to go to Sri Lanka until after I finished writing the book. I've never experienced malnutrition or poverty; but I'd been to Tijuana, Mexico, and Jakarta, Indonesia. I've missed a meal and been hungry. I watched slides and movies and looked at pictures. I entered my imagination and felt what those children were experiencing.

Gloria Kemper once made this statement: "What leaves your head, enters another's head. What leaves your heart, enters another's heart."

You can create an emotional tone, whether you are writing about a place, an emotion, or a tragedy such as suicide. You can make your reader laugh or cry. Create tears in your reader's eyes rather than in the eyes of your characters.

The way to achieve this reader response is to show, don't tell. Show the reader your message through emotions and personal stories. Reach out with your writing and touch the heart of your reader as a young Sri Lankan girl named Lallani has done in the example below from *You Start with One:*

> The day arrived when it was time to say good-bye; our "vacation" in Sri Lanka was at an end. We were not sure when, or if, we would see [Lallani] again....
>
> [Lallani said], "I'm staying home because you are going back to America. I'll never see you again. I must stay with you to the end." I stepped toward her and placed my hands on her shoulders. I felt at a loss for words. I wanted to give her one more thing; but all my trinkets, candy, and gum were gone.
>
> Then I reached in my shirt pocket and pulled out my worn New Testament that I always carried. Over the years, I had underlined it and written in the margins. The pages were crinkled and bent. "Lallani, I want to leave this valuable book with you. Don't let your parents sell it. It tells stories about Jesus."
>
> Lallani nodded her head. Her lower lip quivered.
>
> I swallowed and said, "I will pray for you, Lallani, and for Gongala and your parents, too." A lump formed in my throat. I could not speak. I felt as if I were deserting my own child.
>
> Lallani cried softly. "Never see you again, Uncle."
>
> I put my arms around this special little girl and held her for a moment (pp. 41-42).

There is power in simplicity and personal sharing. Fill your anecdotes with emotion, not abstract ideas. Touching the reader's emotions will help him or her identify with you and the people in your story.

Chapter Three

Where Do You Find Ideas?

The two most engaging powers of an author are to make new things familiar, and familiar things new.

—William Makepeace Thackeray

When I teach classes on writing, I am often asked, "Where do you find ideas?" Many people are afraid they won't have anything to say or they will develop writers' block and find themselves staring at a blank piece of paper. Let me assure you, ideas are all around you—in all you see, hear, taste, touch, feel, or experience in any way.

Finding Ideas

You can draw on your own experiences or those of friends and family members for articles and stories to write. Look around your church for interesting people and unique ministries. Check out your local newspaper, your community, and current world events for even more ideas.

Yourself

The best place to find ideas for articles, stories, and devotionals to write is to look at yourself. What have you experienced that will interest others?

You can draw on past and present events or lessons you have learned. You can state your opinions in something like an op-ed piece or a letter to the editor in your local newspaper or a national magazine.

Have you learned a lesson in coping with a problem or difficult circumstances? Perhaps others can benefit from the road you have walked. A word of caution though: Make sure you are healed before you begin writing, or your anger and unresolved feelings will come out. If you bleed all over the page, no one will benefit.

Consider your hopes and dreams. Share them to encourage others in your personal experience articles.

Do you have any interesting hobbies that others can learn about? Often people's busy schedules or their budgets won't allow them to attend classes. You can be their classroom teacher and show them how to do or make something through a how-to article.

If you keep a journal, some of your entries may provide interesting slices of daily life. If you can write about the mundane in an exciting, humorous way, you will entertain your audience well. Be aware, however, that many of the things in your journal are meant for your eyes only, and others will not benefit from reading about them. Learn to discern what will interest others and what will not.

Sometimes our childhood memories provide interesting anecdotes. Again, be careful that what you experienced is relevant to today's audience.

Often events that happen in the workplace or while you are doing volunteer work provide excellent fodder for stories. One student of mine wrote about her work at a local rescue mission. Another worked at a preschool, and another volunteered her time at a home for unwed mothers. All of these experiences provided excellent material for stories.

Also be sure to keep a journal when you travel. You never know what interesting situation you might encounter. Readers love to go on adventures in cities and countries where they will never travel. They can live vicariously through your exciting adventures, benefiting from the lessons you learned along the way if you make your story realistic.

Some of the incidents in your life will make excellent personal experience stories. Others might give you ideas for short stories. Fiction comes to life when it is based on a true story.

Friends and Family

We can draw on the experiences of our family and friends by interviewing them and, of course, on our experiences with them for more ideas. Two people involved in an incident open the door for dialogue, and nothing moves a story along better than a conversation.

Does your grandmother have a familiar saying that has shaped your life? If so, pass her words of wisdom on to others. Has she led an interesting life that you can capture on paper so her loved ones will have it long after she is gone? What a special legacy to pass on. I regret that my grandmother died before

I had a chance to get her story down on paper. She escaped from Mexico during a revolution; and if I only had more information, I could write a fascinating true story in her memory.

You may have a friend with a totally different viewpoint on a subject than your own. Write a heated debate in dialogue, showing both sides of the situation and voicing both opinions.

Perhaps the story you have in mind contains sensitive information. You never want to hurt your friends and family members with articles that you write, so it is important to handle these situations delicately. You can do one of three things in this instance:

1. Change the name of the person, the place the incident occurred, and perhaps the time of the event. I did this in a devotional I wrote about a girl who tried to commit suicide. I didn't want her or anyone who knew her to recognize the incident, so I changed her name and placed the event three years before it occurred.

2. Change your name, and write the article under a pseudonym. In this case, you would also change the main character's name and some of the circumstances. I find ideas for names in my telephone directory. Using a pseudonym will be discussed in more detail in Chapter 22.

3. Write a fictional story regarding the incident. Again make sure you change enough of the information so your friends and family members don't recognize themselves and feel as if they are part of a soap opera. The nice thing about fiction is you can take the essence of the story and craft it in a way that the reader gains the maximum benefit from the point you are trying to make. You are not hindered by facts. Fiction will be covered in detail in Chapters 17 and 18.

In many cultures, traditions are passed down from generation to generation. If you have such heirlooms, make sure you capture them on paper. Who were your ancestors? How do they affect your life and the lives of your family members today?

Your Church

Does your church have anyone who has done something out of the ordinary? If so, write an interview article about that individual. What about special programs and activities? Perhaps your church sponsors a soup kitchen, a Special Olympics program, or concerts at the park. Church staff members are always looking for articles regarding new outreach programs.

Another place to glean ideas is from your pastor's sermons. For years I was blessed to be pastored by Chuck Swindoll. I was careful not to take the essence of his sermon, for that would be plagiarism. Plus his books are taken from his sermons. However, I would hear a sentence or phrase that would trigger an idea of my own, and I would jot down just enough words so I could write a devotional or article when I had time.

Your Community

When you are reading your local newspaper, watch for interesting people to interview. A word of warning though: Don't contact individuals too close to a tragedy. Allow time for healing. Keep an eye out for special events and current events as well as for interesting people. The newspaper is a wonderful source for fictional stories too. Sometimes truth is stranger than fiction.

As well as searching through your newspaper, you can find ideas in magazines, from radio shows and news briefs, and from television. Documentaries provide a great deal of background for stories and articles, too.

Your World

Anniversaries of historical events bring to mind past happenings and special people who are worth writing about today. Study historical figures and see which ones were Christians. Show how they demonstrated good ethics and values through the choices they made in life.

Landmarks provide another avenue for vicariously transporting the reader to a place he might not visit. Perhaps you can use a landmark as a metaphor in a story. I once wrote a devotional about walking to a lighthouse. I used its beacon as something I wanted to imitate in my own life, so Christ's love would shine brightly through me.

I keep a tablet and pen on the table where I have my morning devotions. Often Scripture triggers an idea for a devotional or a short anecdote. I jot down enough information so I don't forget the idea and then return to my devotions. I do the same thing when I am reading books, magazines, and newsletters. I've even been inspired by advertisements in the newspaper and on TV. Conferences and speeches are also good sources for triggering ideas.

Sometimes inspiration comes in the middle of the night. I think that happens because our subconscious works best when we are quiet. Plus it's been my experience that God doesn't speak very loudly; and if I'm talking or busy with activities, sometimes I don't hear Him. Yet in the middle of the night, He often speaks through my mind. I've learned to get up and jot down the essence of the idea. If I don't, sadly it is gone by morning—never to be recovered again.

Anywhere you go and anything you do can provide ideas for writing. That is why I keep a small tablet and pen in my purse at all times. When an idea strikes, I can easily record the necessary information.

Determining the Value of an Idea

Once you think of an idea, how do you know if it is worth writing about or not? Here are ten questions to ask in measuring the value of an idea:

1. Will your idea interest the reader?
2. Is it significant to the reader's life?
3. Will it meet needs, answer questions, or deal with problems?
4. Does it have universal appeal?
5. Is the idea timely?
6. Do you have a unique twist to your story?
7. Whether true or fictional, is it realistic?
8. Is it something you know and care about?
9. Does it provide take-away value for the reader?
10. Can you find a publication that will buy it?

Once you have determined that an idea is valuable, develop it into an article using the three-step writing method mentioned in Chapter 1.

Ideas are all around you. All you need to do is learn how to recognize them.

Chapter Four

How Do You Find Time to Write?

To love life is to love time. Time is the stuff life is made of.

—Benjamin Franklin

What would you do if every morning a teller from your bank phoned and told you your account had been credited with 86,400 pennies ($864)—but the bank had placed the stipulation on it that you had to spend it that day? No balance could be carried over to the next day. Think of the fantastic things you could do with such a gift.

God credits each of us with 86,400 seconds each day, but no balances are carried into the next day. Each night erases what we fail to use and what we use unwisely. Lost time can't be reclaimed.

If you're having trouble finding enough time to write, try the following time management tips for writers.

Pray before You Begin

It's easy to plunge into something without taking time to talk to God about it, but starting any project with prayer makes your time more productive. Before you begin to write, ask God for wisdom and guidance. If it is His desire that you become an author, He will help you find the necessary time.

Make a Time Commitment

In order to write, you need to plan ahead and set the necessary time aside for it. Perhaps you will decide to write an hour every day, or perhaps you will start with only fifteen minutes if you are a beginning writer. If you can't write every day, try to select a certain day of the week and clear your calendar as best you can.

Use Your Time Wisely

If you want to become an author, you need to treat your writing like a business. Don't wait until the house is spotless or until all the yard chores are done to start writing, or you'll never begin!

If you don't have a writing time currently built into your schedule, decide what activities you can eliminate. Often we can find wasted time or chores that don't need to be done right away. Be careful, however, not to neglect your family and friends. If a friend calls with a problem, don't tell him he's interrupting your writing time. Say "no," however, to anyone who starts a conversation with, "Since you're a writer and don't have to go to the office, I'm sure you'll have time to bake a cake for the PTA, stuff envelopes, or head the new church committee."

Set Writing Goals

What do you want to accomplish in your writing? Dream big, and then divide those ambitions into small goals that are specific and achievable. I do not recommend that beginners start with books. Writing a book is like eating an elephant, and you don't want to end up with indigestion. Begin with articles and stories for magazines and Sunday school take-home papers.

Writing goals should include three things:

1. They must be specific.
2. They need to be measurable.
3. They must have a time factor.

Perhaps a realistic goal would be an article a month. In a year, you would have twelve articles or stories.

Lee Roddy, a well-known fiction author and speaker, challenges writers to produce a page a day. If you do so, in a year you'll have 365 pages which is about two trade-size books. Of course, that doesn't include the time needed for editing.

Remain Flexible

In Chapter 1, I discussed writing goals. Sometimes circumstances change, and your goals must change also. Remain flexible. Unforeseen circumstances can creep into your life.

Stretch yourself so you will grow and learn. Step out in faith and allow God to work through you to accomplish goals that will glorify Him.

Set Aside a Regular Time to Write Each Day

Pick a time when you are most creative and efficient. Writing takes a tremendous amount of energy. If you are home and have small children, that time might be nap time or while they are in school since you'll accomplish more if the house is quiet. If you have a full-time job, perhaps you could find time in the evenings or early mornings. If your house is never quiet, perhaps you could write at the office before or after hours. If you are a night owl, write when everyone else has gone to bed.

Find a Quiet Place to Concentrate

When you write to glorify God, He deserves all your attention. You can't concentrate if the TV is blaring, the phone is ringing, your spouse is talking, or children are screaming. You need to find a place that is free from interruptions.

Can you compose on a typewriter or computer, or do you need to write the first draft longhand? Find what works for you. If you compose with a pen, you could go to a park, a restaurant, or the beach. If you need a laptop computer outlet, go to a library or hotel lobby. Personally, my favorite place to write is in my gazebo at the edge of our property, overlooking a stream and golf course.

Keep Your Body as Well as Your Mind in Shape

If you eat properly, get enough sleep, and exercise regularly, your mind will be sharper and more creative. Also take regular breaks from your writing so you can come back refreshed. Participate in activities with other people, and you will find new subjects to write about.

In order to pull information out of your mind, there has to be a storehouse from which to withdraw it. If you spend all your time writing, you will feel drained. Have you experienced a time when you were pulling more out of your brain than you were putting in? Didn't you feel drained?

Read for pleasure as well as reading research material related to your writing. I suggest spending as many hours reading as you do writing.

Organize Your Work

Keep your home office looking professional. Organize each writing project in a file folder. Label each folder as you obtain ideas for articles or books. What starts out as an article file on dealing with stress may turn into a book five years later. Place everything you find regarding that subject in your file folder.

Keep Accurate Financial Records

Keep a ledger of expenses and income for your writing. Excel and Quicken are excellent Windows computer programs for keeping financial records. If you are making a serious attempt to run a business, you can write off the expenses on your tax return. Get receipts for your postage, office supplies, telephone calls, and dinners with editors. If you drive to an interview or other job-related function, you can deduct mileage.

Also keep track of each submission, noting what is in circulation, where you sent it, and when you mailed it. Keeping accurate records will save you time in the long run.

Avoid Procrastination

Have you heard people say, "I've always wanted to be a writer. I'm going to write when the children grow up, when I retire, when my husband retires. Someday, when I have the time, I'm going to..."? If you are going to become a writer, you need to start writing right *now*.

Write Now!

Writing is ninety-nine percent perspiration and one percent inspiration. It takes a little talent, a strong desire, and a lot of hard work. If you manage your time properly, you will find time to write. Remember what I said at the beginning: God gives us enough hours to do all He wants us to do. We have 86,400 seconds every day. Let's use this time to glorify God in all we do.

Chapter Five

Keeping Your Credibility through Research

The man who doesn't read good books has no advantage over the man who can't read them.

—Mark Twain

A woman once told me at a writers' conference that she wanted to become a fiction writer because she hated research. She said, "If I write fiction, I can just make it up! Then I won't have to spend all that time in stuffy libraries."

Fiction needs to be every bit as accurate as nonfiction. Fiction must be believable—and so must nonfiction for that matter. Do not lose your credibility with your readers by not researching your subject properly.

Research is the process of gathering material from a wide variety of sources. Your writing should reflect a great deal of research so that you write with an abundance of material. Hopefully you will develop far more knowledge on a subject than will be needed to include in an article or book.

Some books and articles take a great deal of research; others draw more on your own experiences. Whether you're writing fiction or nonfiction, however, become knowledgeable about your subject. It is vital to get your facts right and to have every detail accurate.

In the working manuscript of my book, *You Start with One*, I had alligators sunning themselves on the riverbank. A biologist informed me that there are no alligators in Sri Lanka. I changed it to crocodiles before the book went to press.

Author Cecil Murphey lists several errors he recently found in books. One was a World War II novel that mentioned a German Shepherd dog in France. The problem is that on the Continent, people don't refer to them as German Shepherds; they call them Alsatians.

As another example, a woman felt along the wall until she found the light switch. Then she turned it on. This mystery was set in 1922, before wall switches were invented. A biography about a little boy in 1934 stated that when he got a few pennies, he bought a package of Bazooka bubble gum. The problem is that Bazooka is a World War II instrument developed in the '40s.

Do your research carefully so that all your facts will be accurate. You can lose your credibility with your reader if you make a silly mistake.

Primary Research

Primary research is information obtained directly from people, places, or events. This type of research is valuable because it draws you in and makes you, the author, personally involved. It is usually obtained orally. Interviews will be covered in depth in Chapter 13.

People are wonderful resources, and they are usually willing to help an author. Call scientists, policemen, doctors, and college professors—experts in whatever field you are writing about.

Go to your locations and walk where you have your main character walk. Talk to people who have been through a similar experience. Find as many sources as time permits. Once you have been there, the setting will come alive for you. Then use all your senses to paint the scene for the reader.

Secondary Research

Secondary research depends on the printed research found in books, magazines, newspapers, libraries, and museums. A word of caution: Errors can creep in when you depend on others to do your research for you—particularly when you quote someone who is quoting from another source.

Sometimes, however, secondary research is your only option or is necessary to supplement primary research. There are many valuable sources, and research librarians at your local or university library can become your best friends. They love to help you find information.

I checked with the reference librarian at my local library, and these are the main sources he recommended: *Readers' Guide to Periodical Literature*, *Poole's Index to Periodical Literature*, *National Geographic*, and *The New York Public Library Desk Reference*. For quick facts he recommended *Facts on File* books, *Benet's Readers' Encyclopedia*, and *The World Almanac and Book of Facts*. *The New York Times Index* is on microfiche in most libraries and online. *Current Biography Yearbook* and *Who's Who in America* list biographies of prominent public figures and current people in the news.

Historical societies and travel agencies offer helpful brochures and pamphlets. The government printing office offers many free or inexpensive pamphlets, and other government agencies provide publications as well. Churches and synagogues may have historical information available. Plus public relations departments of companies and corporations are wonderful sources for data.

Encyclopedias are now available online and on CD-ROMs. Online services are invaluable. America Online (AOL), CompuServe, and the Worldwide Web offer infinite sources of knowledge. Buy a modem if you don't already own one, and learn how to use these indispensable services.

Online Research

Online research is the perfect answer for the woman I met at the writers' conference who hates stuffy libraries. You don't have to sit in an uncomfortable chair or refrain from eating, drinking, or talking to do your research. You can sit in the comfort of your own home with a mug of steaming coffee, a blazing fire, and soft music in the background.

Steve Laube, an editor and computer expert who often speaks on this subject at writers' conferences, wrote an excellent chapter entitled "Using the Internet for Research" in *A Complete Guide to Writing for Publication* (Susan Titus Osborn, ed., Phoenix: ACW Press, 1999). Much of the following information is taken from his research and used with his permission.

According to Steve, search engines are the key to successful research on the Internet. These are computer programs designed to hunt through a database for the information you want. He suggests, "For best results, use quotation marks around the words in your search query."

For example, if you type "used cars" instead of just "cars" the search engine will trigger all the Web pages that have both "used" and "cars" in their index. The more specific you can make the search, the better. For example, "1967 Mustang convertibles" is even more exact. The more precise you make it, the less hits (possible sources of information) you get, and the easier it will be to go through the material.

Steve lists the most of the major search engines in this chapter as well as tips to maximize their use. Links to search engines and other writers' helps can be found on his Resource for Writers web site at www.acwpress.com/links.htm. (Make sure to order a copy of *A Complete Guide to Writing for Publication*. See the address at the back of this book.)

Beware! Twenty-eight Pitfalls Ahead!

Success comes to a writer as a rule, so gradually that it is always something of a shock to him to look back and realize the heights to which he has climbed.

—P. G. Wodehouse

Writing the first draft is only the beginning of your manuscript. The next step is editing it. When you critique the first draft, watch for the following twenty-eight pitfalls.

Impractical Vocabulary

Don't talk down to your reader, and don't talk above his or her head. *Readers Digest* and *Guideposts* are written on a sixth-grade level. Keep your writing on a parallel level with your reader. Use "ten cent" words rather than ones not commonly used in conversation. You can express profound thoughts and still write in a clear manner.

Unnecessary Words

Eliminate any words, sentences, or paragraphs that don't further your story line. Go through your manuscript word by word and ask yourself, "What will happen if I leave that out? If the answer is "nothing," then cut it.

Unnatural Speech

Your words should flow in a conversational manner as if you were sitting at your dining room table having a cup of tea with a friend. Make your words sound natural. You will be able to do this with practice and lots of rewriting.

Long, Run-on Sentences

If the reader drowns in your sentences, he will feel lost. Keep your writing simple. Doing so doesn't mean the content is simple but the style is. When a sentence is shorter, it usually is stronger. So try to keep your sentences under twenty-five words.

Monotonous Sentences

Have you ever gone to a boring lecture where the speaker droned on in a monotone? Perhaps it was the lecturer's tone that put you to sleep. Since your readers can't hear you, change your tone by varying the length of your sentences. Also vary your sentence structure.

Unclear Material

Sentences that don't flow well can be detected by reading them aloud. Also have someone else read your manuscript and edit it. I cannot emphasize enough the importance of belonging to a critique group. Form one with local writers in your area, and meet regularly.

Incongruities

If you are writing a historical story set during World War II, don't have the characters watch television. It wasn't invented yet. Also, many words came into our vocabulary after World War II. Check to see when a word came into use if there is any doubt in your mind.

Loose Ends

Did you drop a character in your story? If you edit out a character or a piece of furniture, don't let it pop up later. People who aren't as close to your story as you are will be able to see loose ends better than you will.

Digression

Irrelevant material should be eliminated. Remove needless descriptions of people and places. Ask yourself if a scene is necessary. If not, delete it. Use judgment in deciding which characters should be described and in how much detail, what facts are relevant, and what can be left out.

Put-downs

You don't want to offend any element of your audience. Flippant remarks stand out. So watch your own personal prejudices regarding race, gender, and age; and try not to let them creep into your writing. Keep your writing broad based so it will appeal to a wide audience.

Flashbacks

Use flashbacks sparingly, and don't flashback on flashbacks. They are tricky, and you don't want to lose your readers.

Carefully take the readers back to an exact time and place, then bring them forward with good transitions and perhaps some telescoping narrative (covering a long period of time in few words).

Abstract Words and Concepts

Use concrete words instead of abstract ones. Strangely, you may find it more difficult to write simply, in descriptive concrete terms, than to express complex thoughts since people tend to think in the abstract. Put as much detail and description in as is feasible.

Christian Clichés

Don't use Christian jargon that pigeonholes you into one market. Examples include "washed in the blood" and "born-again Christian." Try to avoid any terms that are not found in the Bible. You will find "born again" in the Bible, but you won't find "born-again Christian."

Christianese keeps you from crossing over into denominations other than your own. More importantly, its use keeps you from being effective with non-Christians. Unbelievers often pick up a Christian magazine or book, especially when they are dealing with a problem. Your writing may be able to reach out and touch these individuals and perhaps bring them to Christ. Write so they can understand your words.

Clichés or Jargon

Avoid clichés like the plague, and don't be caught dead using them. They are old hat and will bore your audience to tears. Likewise, don't use shop talk or jargon only understood by one segment of the population, such as legalese and medical terms.

Humdrum Verbs

Use action verbs. The verb is the most important part of the sentence; it moves the reader along. For instance, look at the dynamic verbs for movement starting with the letter *s*: Strut, skip, slink, smash, stomp, slither, stumble, stagger, sashay, swagger, step, stalk, straddle, slip, sneak, steal, slide, shadow, stamp, skid, and stride. Aren't these more exciting than "walk" ?Use dynamic, descriptive verbs.

Use onomatopoeia, words that imitate sounds. These are especially effective when writing for children. Young children love to say words that sound like what they are: Splish, splash, whirl, crash, crunch, smash, toot toot, whee whee, growl, and buzz are examples. Plus, they are all dynamic verbs.

Passive Voice

Keep your sentences in the active voice with the subject doing the acting rather than being acted on. "The car slammed into the man" is more powerful than "The man was hit by the car." This style keeps the readers involved in what is happening.

"To Be" Verbs

Eliminate weak verbs, such as *was, were, is, had, have, become,* and any form of *to be.* Instead of writing, "He is happy," use "He skipped down the road, humming his favorite tune." Often when you eliminate a to be verb, you also get rid of an "ing." For example, instead of saying, "The man was ambling down the road," use "The man ambled down the road."

Negatives

Write in a positive form. Leaving out negative words makes your writing clearer and more upbeat. Also, negatives are often confusing. Example: Instead of saying, "He was not very often on time," use "He usually came late."

Abstract Nouns

Use descriptive nouns. Nouns that are concrete, specific, and definite are best. Instead of "tree," name a type that describes what you want the reader to see, such as eucalyptus, magnolia, or aspen.

Adjectives

Adjectives are necessary, but use them as sparingly as possible. An overdone example is: "The thin, narrow, black ribbon of highway wound through the velvety, emerald-green dense jungle that lurked on either side of the thin, narrow, black ribbon of highway." Instead say: "The narrow ribbon of highway wound through the dense jungle that lurked on either side."

Adverbs

Instead of using a weak verb and an adverb, use a dynamic verb in the past tense. Instead of "walked slowly," use "ambled." By using strong verbs, you can eliminate most adverbs.

Dialogue Tags

"He said" is a perfectly good tag and can be used often. It is usually better than "he uttered," "he articulated," or "he expressed." What matters is what he said, i.e., the words within the quotation marks. You can use an occasional word like whispered, shouted, or asked, but try to keep your tags in dialogue simple. Sometimes you can eliminate them altogether if it is obvious who is speaking.

Noncommittal Language

Avoid tame, colorless, hesitant, noncommittal language. Try not to use such words as *little*, *so*, *very*, *just*, and most *thats*. Keep your readers interested in what you are saying by the way you say it.

Preachy Words

Use words like *would*, *should*, *could*, *may*, *might*, and *can* sparingly. If you preach to your audience, you will lose them.

Jesus didn't tell people what to do. Instead, He spoke in parables. He used anecdotal stories to get His points across to His audience. Try using that same technique.

Missing Punctuation

Make sure your commas are in the right places and that none have been left out. Do you have a period or other punctuation at the end of each sentence? A good reference for proper punctuation is *Elements of Style.*

Cumbersome Punctuation

Be careful not to over punctuate with commas. Today we use fewer commas than in the past. Also avoid the overuse of dashes, exclamation points, semicolons, and colons.

Poor Transitions

Your paragraphs must flow into each other. If the transition seems rough, add an introductory clause or phrase to smooth it out. "After several hours of traveling, we arrived," or "When we reached Phoenix, we were greeted by our host."

Telling

Show, don't tell. On first rough drafts, writers often tell the story in narrative either from an observer's viewpoint or from the main character's mind. Both of these locations are boring. Readers want to participate in the action. They want to join in the excitement and experience the events as they are happening.

Be concrete, specific, and definite. Use dialogue, anecdotes, and fictional techniques whether you are writing fiction or non-fiction. When we avoid these twenty-eight pitfalls, we make our writing come alive to reach our readers and touch their lives.

It Was a Dark and Stormy Beginning

Writing is easy. All you do is sit staring at a blank piece of paper until the drops of blood form on your forehead.

—Gene Fowler

There are many ways to begin a manuscript. Here are eight suggestions, taken from two of my books. These types of leads apply for devotionals and other short pieces, fiction and nonfiction stories, articles, and book chapters.

Eight Ways to Begin a Story or Article

Narrative

As I scanned the horizon, my eyes focused on a sailboat gliding out of the bay. It cruised smoothly for a moment until the sailor lost the direction of the wind. The mainsail flapped in the breeze, and the boat slowed to a near halt. The man turned the rudder and leaned his craft back into the wind. The sails caught the breeze, and soon the vessel glided swiftly out of the harbor (*Rest Stops for Single Mothers*, p. 47).

Narrative is used to tell a mini-story from the narrator's viewpoint. In the above example, you can picture the sailboat catching the wind.

Characterization

Pushing the gas pedal against the floorboard, the proud eighteen-year-old owner of a beat-up 1929 Ford sped along a dirt road that transversed dusty bean fields. His brown hair was slicked back with a wave, and his blue eyes stared straight ahead. The acres of weeds stretching before him would someday shudder beneath the earsplitting runway traffic of the vast complex known as Los Angeles International Airport (*Eyes Beyond the Horizon*, p. 31).

Characterization is often used as a lead. This description of Bob Bowman gives the reader an insight into his looks and personality as a teen. The description of the scene transports the reader back to L.A. in the 1930's.

Thesis

Stepping out on a venture of faith is like being propelled swiftly down an unknown path in the dark. There is confidence and excitement instead of fear. If the way leads suddenly over the edge of a cliff, faith says the foot will find support if God underwrites the venture (*Eyes Beyond the Horizon*, p. 45).

A thesis is presented by this lead, which explains a venture of faith. Also, a metaphor is used, comparing stepping out in faith to walking down an unknown path. Antithesis is another vehicle found here. Confidence and excitement are contrasted with fear. Falling over the edge of a cliff is contrasted with being sure-footed.

Problem

My manager at the telephone company, where I worked as a service representative, called me into his office. "I just received a call from White River, Arizona. Your father didn't show up at work today, Susan. He is missing. His car was found parked on a mountain road—empty."

I collapsed into a chair. A small voice inside told me my father was dead (*Rest Stops for Single Mothers*, p. 67).

Presenting a problem to be solved is an excellent way to begin a story. It reaches out and grabs the reader.

Dialogue

"Mom, I had to abandon my car," my son's voice sounded breathless on the other end of the telephone line. "Flames were jumping across the highway. Burning branches fell into the back of my convertible."

"Are you OK?" I asked, concern filling my voice (*Rest Stops for Single Mothers*,p. 103).

Dialogue is an excellent vehicle for jumping into the action of a story. Here it is used in conjunction with the presentation of a problem to be solved.

Mood

Staring out my hotel window on this winter's day in Washington D.C., I watched huge chunks of ice lazily drift

down the Potomac River. I rubbed my arms and shivered—
partly from the cold, but mostly from the memory forming
in my mind (*Rest Stops for Single Mothers*, p. 190).

A mood set by using such phrases as "stared out the window," "huge chunks of ice," and "shivered."

Question

The front door was slammed angrily with a thud. My
son stomped down the stairs and out of earshot. Only
silence remained.

Why do I fight with my son? My stomach churned as I
pondered this question(*Rest Stops for Single Mothers*, p. 110).

A question may be asked at the beginning or near the
beginning of the story or chapter.

Quotation

He who cannot forgive others breaks the bridge over
which he himself must pass. —Author Unknown (*Rest
Stops for Single Mothers*, p. 122).

A quotation may be used to begin a devotional, a story or
article, or a book chapter.

Whatever vehicle you choose for your beginning, make sure
you grab the reader's attention immediately. Don't be afraid to
jump into the action.

Titles with Pizzazz

The title of your article or story is as important as its beginning. The title is what you use to hook the reader, so it must be
eye-catching. Many readers buy a magazine because an article

title piqued their interest. Some readers thumb through a magazine, checking titles and read only the articles for which the title grabbed their attention.

Titles need to be accurate. They should express specifically what will follow in the article. The reader doesn't want to feel cheated because he thought he was getting something totally different than what your article delivered. If your subject matter is serious, make your title serious too. For example, "A Cry for Acceptance." If your material is humorous, you can make the title funny, i.e., "Turning Frogs into Princes."

Titles are usually concise. A good rule is to keep your titles five to seven words. Use active verbs, specific nouns, and descriptive adjectives to grab the reader. Also try to draw in the reader, so he feels actively involved in your article. He needs to feel there is something in it for him. *Stories for the Heart* is a good example.

To create a good title, look for key phrases that seem to sum up the article. Watch for sentences that catch your eye as you read through—perhaps they will captivate your reader too. I wrote an article about a man who escaped from Vietnam. He felt his escape was made possible by God's providential hand, so I named the article, "The Providential Escape."

Another way to catch the reader's attention is by reversing words or changing one word in a common saying to create your own saying. "Forget and Forgive" is a devotional I wrote on forgiveness. Using "Forgive and Forget" would be overuse of a tired cliché. "Take This Job and Love It" is another example of a good play on words.

If you are writing a mystery, use words that show intrigue. *Anonymous Tip* and *Final Witness* are book titles that do this well. The reader wonders, *Who will be the final witness?* Be careful, however, not to tell too much in the title. "John Overcomes Cancer to Win the Race" probably doesn't leave much for the reader to learn from reading the story.

Titles should be easy to pronounce, yet have pizzazz. The more memorable your title, the more apt your article is to be read and remembered. *Experiencing God* is an excellent example that is simple, memorable, and meet's the reader's needs.

Put a lot of thought in a title before sending your manuscript to an editor. The first person you need to impress is her, so she will publish your article or story.

Chapter Eight

Twelve Dynamic Endings

I don't like to write, but I love to have written.

—Michael Kanin

Next to your beginning, your ending is the most important part of your article or story. Here are twelve suggested types of endings with examples taken from my books.

Anecdotal Ending

You can end with an anecdote, which is a short story within a story or article. Or you can use the split-anecdote technique where you start the anecdote in the beginning (or in the middle somewhere) and complete it in the closing.

Looking back over the past ten years, I never dreamed my life would take the path it has. When all I had to hold onto was a thread linking me to God, I learned to step out in faith and to take risks. If I had not been forced to earn a living, I never would have developed my current programs and ministries. After six years of being a single parent, I am now blessed with a supportive husband and a thriving business *(Rest Stops for Single Mothers,* p. 229).

Natural Close

Let your story end naturally. You've told your story. Stop and say no more.

When Mobin visits foreign cities, as he was doing that day in the Maldive Islands, he still tells people, "I collect telephone directories. Do you have one I can take home with me?" *(Potpourri of Praise,* p. 44).

Summary Close

This ending attempts to cover the highlights of the story or article or to tie up all the loose ends.

How wrong my first impression had been. I was aware that God planned that therapeutic evening. He knew I would run out of wood, and although I hadn't specifically asked Him for more, He provided anyhow *(Rest Stops for Single Mothers,* p. 86).

Straight Statement Close

This closing is often used for editorials. It consists of a few sentences or a final thought in the author's own words.

I needed to allow others to be themselves. When I dated someone, I tried to accept him for who he was—not for who I wanted him to be. Through this time, I always felt

God had someone special planned for me. When I was ready, and my "Mr. Perfect"was ready, God would allow us to meet *(Rest Stops for Single Mothers*, p. 152).

Word of Advice Close

This warning or word of advice points a verbal finger at the reader, so be careful not to preach when you use it.

Loving too much leaves us open to the danger of being hurt, but loving too little can cause us to forget how to love and forget how to live *(Rest Stops for Single Mothers*, p. 191).

Stinger

This unexpected conclusion provides an ending that startles, surprises, or shocks the reader.

Elbows jabbed their ribs; feet tangled with theirs; the unrelenting mob moved on until they came to the place where the old man lay. Bending down, they touched the old man's arm, now grown cold. They were too late *(Potpourri of Praise*, p. 178).

Add-on

This close can make a point never made in the story—a shocker or something that seems natural for making your final point. Make sure it doesn't appear tacked on though.

As we walked toward the refreshment table together, I realized that my lack of forgiveness had cost us both a great price *(Rest Stops for Single Mothers*, p.124).

Quote Close

Use a quotation taken from a person, book, historical event, or other source of quotations to add finality to the article.

Angelic flames of light and heavenly choirs, accompanied by celestial harps and trumpets, turned a scene of earthly tragedy into a scene of heavenly triumph. From what they saw that day, and from 'God's Carvings,' the Aucas learned what the Psalmist wrote: "Precious in the sight of the Lord is the death of His saints (Psalm 116:15) (*Potpourri of Praise*, p.22).

Lead Replay

This closer is a duplication or a rewrite of the lead sentence or paragraph or a restatement of the lead's theme.

With the Lord leading the way, FEBC expands its ministry to move to the future as it lifts its eyes beyond the horizon" (*Eyes Beyond the Horizon*, p. 182).

Proximity Close

Tap the material immediately preceding your final paragraph and tie it into that paragraph for a closing.

Next time you are in a church, look carefully at the stained glass windows. Picture yourself as part of His magnificent stained glass window. Watch the sun piercing through each unique piece of glass. Notice how many shapes and sizes are necessary to form the whole.

Remember that the Master Craftsman started with one—one piece of fractured glass. What can we accomplish for His glory if we, too, start with one? (*You Start with One*, p. 143).

Restatement of Purpose

Occasionally, a vivid and colorful restatement of the article's purpose makes an effective close.

God teaches us to pray specifically. He knew that car was important to Rich's education, so He spared it. With what took place, I learned an important lesson: When things look bleakest, God is there, showing His presence in the smallest details of our lives (*Rest Stops for Single Mothers*, p. 104).

Play on Words

Sometimes alliteration, a clever slogan, or a catchy phrase helps your words to stay in the reader's mind.

Pastor Ananda's burden for his flock, however heavy, is carried with joy and compassion. It fits him well. Each of us has our own divinely designed yoke—our own job to do. Suddenly I felt a renewed strength to wear the yoke God has fashioned for me (*Potpourri of Praise*, p.3).

Whatever ending you choose, give your article or story a solid conclusion. Don't just let your story die. Try to come up with an interesting twist so the reader will ask, "Why didn't I think of that?"

Provide the reader with food for thought that he can digest and use in his own life to move closer to the Lord as well as to reach out to help others.

To Comma or Not to Comma

The comma, which seems to cup the sense of the preceding phrase and hold it out to us, timidly and respectfully, is one of our greatest breakthroughs. The civilizing influence of this punctuational aid derives partly from its odd shape, the shape of mosquito larvae and sea horses: close inspection reveals the implied high culture of its asymmetrical tapering swerve, so distinctly an advance over the more rustic period.

—Nicholson Baker

The punctuation error that seems to occur most often in the hundreds of manuscripts crossing my desk each year is misuse of the comma. It is important to learn when to use and when not to use commas. To make matters worse, *The Chicago Manual of Style*, *The Associated Press Handbook*, and grammar books list different rules. Most Christian publishers have their own style sheets, but they basically follow *The Chicago Manual of Style*, which is the standard in the book publishing industry. Since it is costly, I suggest you buy Strunk and White's *The Elements of Style* to help you with grammar, punctuation, and word usage. First copyrighted in 1935, this inexpensive, little book has been updated twice and is packed with all the basics.

Uses of the Comma

Now let's look at some basic rules regarding commas.

Independent Clauses

Always place a comma before a conjunction introducing an independent clause. In other words, place a comma between two independent clauses separated by a conjunction. Independent clauses have a subject and a verb, and they can stand alone. For example: *The situation looked hopeless, but there was one remaining chance for success.* Or *The situation looked hopeless, but I didn't believe it.*

However, do not join independent clauses with a comma if they are lacking a conjunction. They need to be joined with a semicolon, or they can be cut into two separate sentences: *The situation looked hopeless; there was one remaining chance for success.* or *The situation looked hopeless. There was one remaining chance for success.*

A common mistake made with the comma is to separate a dependent clause from an independent clause when they are joined with a conjunction: *I was told the situation looked hopeless but didn't believe it.* Each clause must have a subject in order to need a comma before the conjunction.

According to *The Chicago Manual of Style*, when listing three items a comma is placed after the first and second items: *Paper, pen, and writer all go together.* Some publishers omit the second comma, but they won't fault you for not knowing their style. The important point is to be consistent, so the editor can match the style sheet to your manuscript. Plus, if the lists contain multiple words, it can be confusing if you don't add the second comma: *His pets consisted of a long-haired cat, a short-haired dog, and a very noisy parrot.*

The exception to this rule concerns the name of businesses such as law firms. These usually omit the last comma: *Dewey, Sokum and Howe is a new law firm in town.*

To further complicate things, if the list of items includes commas, they should be set off by semicolons: *The blank, white sheet of paper; the black, fine-line pen; and inspiration are the tools of a writer.*

Parenthetical Material

Another use of the comma is to enclose parenthetic material. Words that can safely be left out without affecting the meaning of the sentence are considered parenthetical. For example: *My son, you will be pleased to know, is now living in Beverly Hills.* Or *My son, Richard, is now living in Beverly Hills.*

A name or a title in direct address is parenthetic and is always set off by commas: *Richard, when are you coming home for a visit?*

No comma should separate a noun from a restrictive term of identification: *William the Conqueror, Richard the Lion-hearted.*

Along with nonrestrictive clauses, clauses introduced by conjunctions indicating time and place are also parenthetic. Consequently, these need a comma: *In 1941, when Pearl Harbor was bombed, I had not been born.*

The word *which* is often used to set off a nonrestrictive clause: *My dog, which is black and furry, is named Kavic.* It does not matter that my dog is black and furry; that description is irrelevant. Go on a "which hunt" to see how many "whiches" should be turned into "thats."

Restrictive clauses are not parenthetic and are not set off by commas. They are necessary to the meaning of the sentence: *The group who sat in the back cheered loudest of all.* The word *that* is often used to introduce a restrictive clause: *The houses that were located in the woods were in danger of catching on fire.* All the houses were not in danger of the fire, only the ones located in the woods. It changes the meaning of the sentence to eliminate "in the woods." The word *that* can often be omitted without hurting the meaning of the sentence as is possible here: *The houses located in the woods were in danger of catching on fire.*

Adverbial Phrases/Clauses

When the main clause of a sentence is preceded by a phrase or a subordinate clause, you may use a comma to separate the phrase: *Sitting in the back, the group cheered wildly.* Or *During the performance, the group cheered wildly.*

If the interruption to the flow of the sentence is slight, however, the comma may be omitted. The comma is usually omitted after short, introductory phrases: *On Tuesday Bill was absent from class.*

An adverbial phrase or clause located between the subject and the verb, however, should be set off by commas: *Bill, after picking up his assignment, went home.*

Commas should be used to set off interjections, transitional adverbs, and similar elements that effect a distinct break in the continuity of thought: *On the other hand, Bill may be right.* Or *Yes, Bill was right after all.*

Adjectives

For clarity, separate two or more adjectives with commas if each modifies the noun alone: *Kavic is a fantastic, faithful dog.* Or *It is going to be a long, hot summer.*

Placement

When a comma is called for at the end of material enclosed in quotation marks, parentheses, or brackets, it should be placed inside the quotation marks but outside the parentheses or brackets. *Bill replied, "Yes," when asked if he'd like to go.* Or *Bill's comment, though stilted (and somewhat inflammatory), was still taken to heart.*

Good Word Usage

Here are some other elementary rules of usage.

Possessive

Form the possessive singular of nouns by adding an *s*: *Mary's house, Charles's farm.*

Exceptions are the possessives of ancient proper names ending in *s*, i.e., *Moses' and Jesus'.*

Possessives, such as *hers, yours,* and *its,* have no apostrophe: *The shade stunted its growth.* *It's* is the contraction for *it is*: *It's now growing in the sun.*

Dash

A dash is a mark of separation stronger than the comma. It is often used for emphasis, but only use when a comma seems inadequate: *He heard someone cry out—an ear-piercing scream.* Do not overuse dashes.

Subject/Verb Agreement

The number of the subject determines the number of the verb. If the subject is singular, the verb must also be singular. Use a singular verb form after *each, either, everyone, everybody, neither, nobody,* and *someone: Someone left her purse in the grocery cart.*

Participles

A participial phrase at the beginning of the sentence must refer to the grammatical subject. Be careful not to leave your participles dangling. *On arriving in Atlanta, I discovered my luggage was missing.* Arriving refers to me and not to my luggage. It would be wrong to say the following because my luggage never arrived: *Upon arriving in Atlanta my luggage was missing.*

For other tips to help you with grammar, punctuation, and word usage, consult *The Chicago Manual of Style* or *The Elements of Style.* The tips in this chapter conform to their standards.

Chapter Ten

Shaping Your
Article or Story

The difference between the almost right word and the right word is really a large matter—'tis the difference between the lightning bug and lightning.

—Mark Twain, *The Art of Authorship*

One of my favorite events to attend is the Rose Parade. I love to watch the beautiful, flower-covered floats move down Colorado Boulevard. in Pasadena, California, each New Year's Day. Each float is uniquely crafted and designed, with each flower carefully selected for a certain location. While watching the parade, all I notice is the beautiful flowers; but they aren't the most important part of the float. The wooden frame underneath is what gives each float structure.

Likewise your articles and stories must have a supportive structure under your well-chosen and polished words. The reader doesn't see the framework, but it must be there. There are two frameworks I use for all my writing, whether articles, stories, devotionals, or books.

These are models in the shape of a spool and a prism designed by my friend and co-author, Christine Harder Tangvald, and reprinted with her permission. These shapes can be used at both the outlining stage of writing (Step 1) and editing and fine-tuning of your article or story (Step 3). (See Chapter 1 for more information on these steps.)

The Shape of the Spool

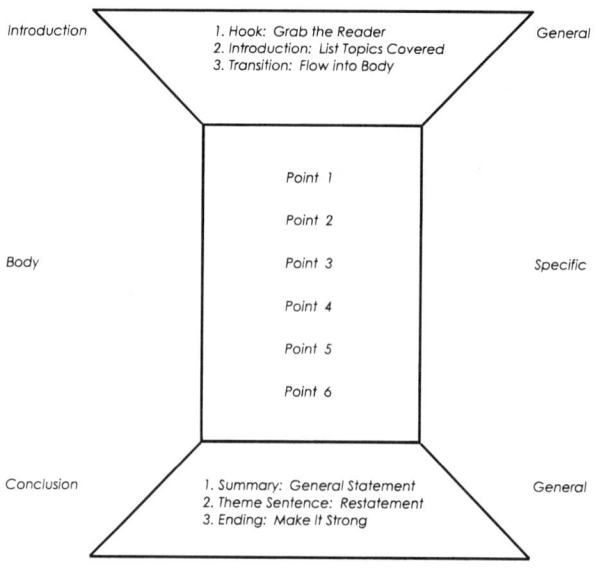

State Theme in One Sentence:

Introduction — General
1. Hook: Grab the Reader
2. Introduction: List Topics Covered
3. Transition: Flow into Body

Body — Specific
Point 1
Point 2
Point 3
Point 4
Point 5
Point 6

Conclusion — General
1. Summary: General Statement
2. Theme Sentence: Restatement
3. Ending: Make It Strong

Focus! Focus! Focus!
Write a Clever Title
All Points Must Relate to the Theme

The shape of a spool is usually used for nonfiction articles, nonfiction books, and some picture books. As with anything you write, the first step is to state your theme in one sentence. Then create an outline, using the shape of a spool. Then use the spool to form and fine-tune your article.

Your article should contain three parts: an introduction, a body, and a conclusion. Your introduction should be general. Grab the reader's interest with your opening sentence. Then list the topics to be covered before transitioning smoothly into the main section of the article.

The body covers your main points and gives the specifics in detail. Each one of your points must relate to the general theme. So be sure your article stays on target without deviating from your premise. Digression is the main problem with the majority of rejected articles. The writer tries to tell too many stories in one article.

Be careful that your theme sentence isn't tacked on the end. Instead, interweave your message throughout the entire article.

The conclusion summarizes with a general statement and/or restates the theme sentence. Make the ending strong. Don't let your article die at the end. Try to include an unusual twist if possible. Next to the opening paragraph, the ending is the second most important part of your article. Last, but not least, write a clever title. Even if the editor changes it, you want to grab him with your idea.

Below is an example of the spool shape which was published May 18, 1997, in *The Upper Room.*

Tongues of Fire
by Susan Titus Osborn

They saw what seemed to be tongues of fire that sepa-
rated and came to rest on each of them. All of them

73

were filled with the Holy Spirit and began to speak in other languages.—Acts 2:3,4 (NIV)

One of my favorite ways to spend an evening is to relax in my recliner by the fireside. I never cease to be amazed at the results when I take a tiny match and touch it to a piece of wadded up paper, placed under kindling and logs. The edges of the paper burn, and soon pieces of dry wood light up with orange-red tongues of fire. The flames spread and the heat builds. The larger logs start to burn. Soon a small spark has become a roaring fire.

Almost 2,000 years ago, God lit a match in Palestine. On the day of Pentecost, only a small number were touched and warmed by the spark of the Good News. Then the flame spread out of Jerusalem and into the Roman Empire. The fire kept growing until today millions of people around the world know Jesus and worship Him.

Fire symbolizes God's purifying presence, which burns away all the undesirable elements of our lives. Perhaps that is why a warm fire relaxes my body and calms my spirit.

Yet fire also represents the Holy Spirit igniting us with courage and wisdom as He did the early Christians on the day of Pentecost. I pray that the Holy Spirit will light a fire in me so I may be a spark to touch and warm a hurting world.

PRAYER: Dear Lord, please work through me as your spark to reach out and ignite a fire within others. In Jesus' name. Amen.

See if you can form an outline for the above devotional. What would your focus sentence be?

The Shape of a Prism

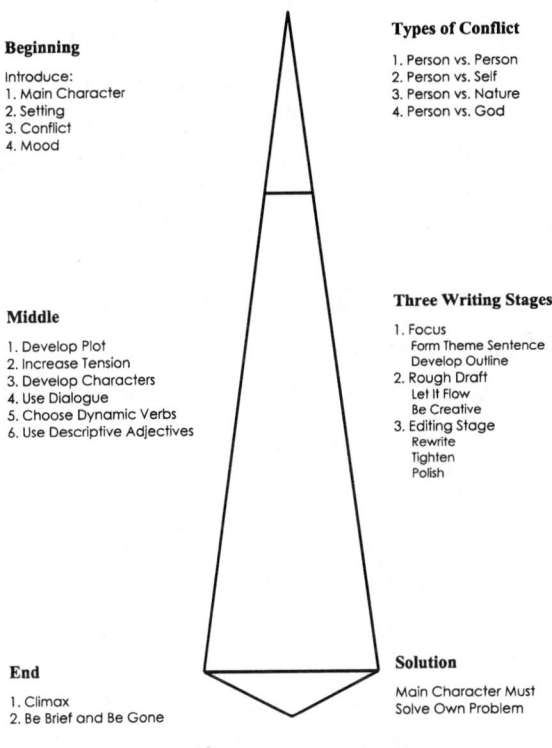

Beginning

Introduce:
1. Main Character
2. Setting
3. Conflict
4. Mood

Types of Conflict

1. Person vs. Person
2. Person vs. Self
3. Person vs. Nature
4. Person vs. God

Middle

1. Develop Plot
2. Increase Tension
3. Develop Characters
4. Use Dialogue
5. Choose Dynamic Verbs
6. Use Descriptive Adjectives

Three Writing Stages

1. Focus
   Form Theme Sentence
   Develop Outline
2. Rough Draft
   Let It Flow
   Be Creative
3. Editing Stage
   Rewrite
   Tighten
   Polish

End

1. Climax
2. Be Brief and Be Gone

Solution

Main Character Must
Solve Own Problem

© Christine Harder Tangvald
Used by Permission - Susan Titus Osborn

The second shape uses the model of a prism. This shape works well for the true personal experience story as well as for fiction, including short stories and novels. It also can be used at both the outlining stage of writing (Step 1) and the editing of your own work (Step 3).

When writing your story, form a focus sentence before you begin. This is the glue that holds the entire story together. Also write a rough outline, although it may change as the story unfolds. Then write a running synopsis which will form the backbone for your story to give it the necessary structure.

Short stories and novels have a beginning, a middle, and an end. That may seem obvious, but many that cross my desk don't! When creating your synopsis, write the beginning and the end before you go back and fill in the middle. You will probably make changes as you go along, but you need to have a plan. It's helpful to know what your climax and ending will be before you actually write the story.

When writing the first draft, find a block of time so your thoughts can flow without any interruption. Don't worry about grammar, punctuation, or phraseology. Just get your story down. If you think of small details as you go, include them. Don't think about your construction or the synopsis you prepared while creating this first rough draft. Leave yourself free from constraints so your creative juices can flow. Personal experience stories and fiction stories both need good continuity. And the better your first draft is, the less work will be required later.

When you rework the first paragraph of your story, remember to hook the reader. Open with an exciting beginning that makes the reader want to read on. Beginnings are covered in detail in Chapter 7.

Your characters need to appear real, whether they are actual people or not. Your characters must seem real to you, or they will never seem lifelike to your readers.

Second, paint a scene. Where are you? Can we picture the location? Does the reader feel that he is actually there? Use all your senses, so the reader can live the experience with you. If you are painting a beach scene, hear the thunder of the waves crashing on the shore. Taste the salt from the spray. Smell the clean, crisp air. Feel the soft breeze brushing across your face.

Then introduce a problem and set the mood of your story. Have only one conflict. In a novel, you can keep introducing complication upon complication, solving some as you go along. In a short story, however, keep it simple. Build suspense; don't give away the ending too soon.

Surprise the reader. After you reach the climax in your story, be brief and be gone. Wrap it up as quickly as possible, but try to provide an interesting twist. Short stories will be covered in detail in Chapter 16.

Here is an example of the prism shape from a devotional in *Still Moments* (Mary Beckwith, compiler, Ventura, CA: Regal Books, 1989).

A Fork in the Road
by Susan Titus Osborn

I gripped my son's hand tightly as we hiked along the path through the towering redwoods. The massive trees shut out most of the sunlight. A light fog made the trail difficult to see.

Suddenly, we came to a fork in the road. My son asked, "Which way do we go, Mom?" His eyes conveyed trust. He assumed I knew the direction out of the woods, but I was caught up in listening to him and hadn't paid attention to where we had walked.

I paused for a moment and thought of how often forks in the road of life confront us. Frequently, when met by a fork, I have made split-second decisions that have affected my entire life. How different my experience might have been had I chosen other paths.

Yet our decisions need not be made alone. God wants us to consult Him concerning even the smallest decisions in life. Through prayer and reading the Scriptures, we can stay in tune with God's direction for our lives.

I looked down one fork of the trail, which divided the world's tallest living trees. Then I gazed down the other. In the distance I saw a faint amber light, which I recognized as the sign on top of the mountain cabin resort where we were staying. With confidence I said, "This is the right path. Let's go."

People are searching for adventure. They want to escape from today's problems. Yet often they need help learning to deal with or overcoming these obstacles. Stories, whether real or fictional, make excellent vehicles for meeting the reader's real need as well as his or her felt need.

Chapter Eleven

The Sure-sell Magazine Article

I desire never to converse with a man who has written more than he has read.

—Samuel Johnson

Most people want to write books. Yet, magazine articles can reach far more people to touch many lives. A personal experience story in *Guideposts* reaches 4-5 million people. A testimony in *Decision* reaches 1.7 million people. A current social issue article in *Discipleship Journal* reaches 90,000. A family issue article in *Christian Parenting Today* reaches 250,000 homes. By comparison, a first run on a book is usually between 5,000-10,000.

Here are some of the types of articles you can write.

Personal Experience Articles

Personal experiences continue to be the most popular magazine articles. This is the type of story used in *Guideposts*, although a number of other Christian publications use personal experience stories too. These are usually written from interviews. I recommend using a tape recorder as well as taking notes while interviewing people. They don't have to be celebrities, but they need to be interesting individuals with whom your audience will identify. Make sure the reader will glean some take-away value from the article to use in his or her own life.

Also you can write your own testimony or a personal experience story about one incident in your life. Have the courage to be open and honest with your reader. On the other hand, don't air your dirty laundry or hurt family members or acquaintances. *Decision* buys testimonies. often in short versions called vignettes. Personal experience articles will be covered extensively in Chapter 12.

Current Social Issues Articles

Current issues manuscripts address today's problems with biblical values and answers. Some of these are AIDS, teen pregnancy, divorce, abortion, drug and alcohol abuse, health care, runaways, suicide, and cleaning up the environment. Choose issues you feel passionately about for your articles. Look at how the Christian community is responding to your particular topic. Obtain information from experts who will give credibility to your work.

Today's writing is moving from the didactic to the anecdotal. Include personal experience stories in these articles as vignettes if the article isn't already written in the personal experience format.

Issue articles are a good way to cross over into the secular market. Start with an article in your local newspaper. If you quote Scripture in a secular newspaper or magazine, you are eligible to enter the article in the prestigious Amy Awards with first prize of $10,000.

Art of Living Articles

This type of article includes inspirational essays and narrative, articles on faith and religion, and self-help articles (which will be dealt with separately). As a group, these are the staple of most general-interest magazines and represent a good market for new writers. Inspirational articles deal with our inner world of personal feelings. This kind of writing tends to surprise the reader by taking an old, forgotten truth and revealing it in a fresh, new way. It's been said that the obvious is that which is never understood until someone expresses it in a simple, concrete manner. The purpose of art-of-living articles is to make a difference in people's lives.

How-to Articles

How-to articles explain how to build or make something, how to solve a problem, or how to improve yourself. If you can write articles telling others a faster or easier way to accomplish something, you will find a wide-open market waiting for you. Many people can't attend classes, so they pick up magazines and newspapers to learn how to make, build, or be.

Self-help Articles

This type focuses on psychological benefits rather than on products used. The material objects involved are secondary. In these you try to motivate a change in the reader's attitude, which makes him feel better or helps him develop a better attitude. Many of the issues dealt with are the same as in a personal experience article. "You can overcome, cope, manage, survive—if you follow my suggestions" is the message given. Provide a wealth of solid information backed by careful research to add credibility to your article.

Devotionals

Many magazines publish devotionals. Plus there are a number of devotional guides in print, such as *The Upper Room*. Again, your experiences or those of others make excellent material. These are usually 250 words. Write tightly, because every word counts. Writing devotionals will be discussed further in Chapter 14.

Shorts and Fillers

Short pieces are another wonderful way to break into new markets with few words. Sally Stuart's *Christian Writers' Market Guide* (published annually by Harold Shaw) has eight pages of publications listed according to categories that publish fillers. For example, *Guideposts* has a short column called "This Thing Called Prayer." Many publishers use fillers when they find a small space at the bottom of a column or page that needs to be filled.

Holiday Articles

Seasonal articles are another way to break into new markets. Most publications looking for seasonal material want Christmas, Easter, or Thanksgiving; but avoid Santa Claus and Easter Bunnies. Also, you might consider lesser-known holidays as well as anniversaries of events that could be given a religious twist, i.e., the Berlin wall coming down, Vietnam Memorial, Pearl Harbor. Submit material at least nine months in advance.

Church School Take-home Papers

Take-home papers are another excellent market for which you can write all of the above articles. Many denominational publishing houses as well as nondenominational houses publish them. Issues are printed fifty-two times a year, and many houses publish them for all age groups. Most don't require a query letter. For example, the *Lookout* is sixteen pages with a circulation of 118,000. Be sure to write for a theme list when writing for guidelines.

Study the *Christian Writers' Market Guide*, and write for guidelines and a sample issue before you begin to write your article. Slant it for a particular publication. Then sit down and write the sure-sell magazine article.

Touching Lives with Personal Experience Articles

Tell a story! Don't try to impress your reader with style or vocabulary or neatly turned phrases. Tell the story first!

—Anne McCaffrey

Everyone has a story to tell. We all have at least one story inside our heads. You can use your own personal experiences to create salable articles or use interviewing techniques to tell the stories of others.

Do you know what type of magazine article is the most popular? It is the inspirational, true-life drama—the personal experience story.

Do you keep a journal? This is an excellent way to get your feelings down on paper, but remember that some of the entries in your journal are meant just for you. These entries have been therapeutic for you to put down on paper, but they won't benefit others. Remember, when you are writing for publication, you are writing for your reader not for yourself. And you don't ever want to bore your reader.

Richard Green, formerly with *Decision*, suggests three excellent questions to ask yourself before you begin writing your story:

1. What have I learned from this experience?
2. What can I teach others through what I have learned?
3. What do I want the reader to do at the end of the article?

In a personal experience article, the story line becomes the vehicle to relate the message you want to convey to the reader. It may be a moral lesson, an ethical issue, or a religious truth. You want to provide insight and instruction for your reader. He must learn to *own* his own belief system and values to live by. In order for the reader to identify with your story, the humanness of your main character needs to come through clearly. If you are writing your story, then you are the main character.

Consequently, you must become vulnerable with your reader and be willing to make yourself transparent. Be careful not to air your dirty laundry though. Try to chat with your reader as if she were a friend, sitting at your kitchen table sharing a cup of tea. Try to be open and honest, so the reader can benefit from your experience.

Your personal experience story must have a beginning, a middle, and an end. You must present a problem, show conflict, and come to a resolution. Refer to Chapter 10, and use the shape of a story for your personal experience article.

The best plumb line to use when writing the personal experience story is *Guideposts*, a top-selling Christian magazine with more than five million subscribers. I suggest you write to *Guideposts* for their guidelines and use them as a guide for other

Christian publications that accept first-person, personal experience stories. In the secular market, *Readers Digest,* is the plumb line.

The personal experience story is about 1200-1500 words and is always true. It is usually written in the first person because it is more powerful. It contains three ingredients.

Ingredients

Reader Identification

The reader may not have experienced exactly the same thing but he can empathize. You want the reader to be involved at the heart level. Write heart to heart, not head to head. You want to work a change in your reader's heart that will result in a change in his life. Be careful not to preach but involve the reader on an emotional level. You do this by using fictional techniques in your nonfiction—anecdotes, dialogue, and description. Be specific and concrete, not abstract. Take the reader on a journey with you. Make him feel and see all that is happening on the way.

You want him to say, "I couldn't put the story down. I cried. I laughed." This reaction is achieved by showing the reader, rather than telling him. Remember, show—don't tell.

Take-away

The take-away is what the reader remembers when he has forgotten the story, what she takes from your story and uses in her life to become a better person, to move closer to God, or to realize a truth.

Spiritual Emphasis or Reader's Reaction

Move your reader, inspire him, arouse his emotions. You want the reader to do something when he finishes reading your story. Perhaps you want him to change in some way or to desire to help another individual.

Write in an interesting style, presenting a new twist. Your story must have appeal and drama. Tell what the problem is and how to solve it. You don't want the editor to say, "Didn't I just read that story half an hour ago?"

Keep your story upbeat. As Christians, we live victoriously. Most publications want a happy ending and some kind of a turnaround; the story needs to go somewhere.

Possible Subjects

Now let me offer eight subjects for personal experience stories presented by author Kathy Collard Miller and used with her permission.

Physical healing

This topic can include healing of actual physical injuries, recovering from an illness, or recovering from an addiction.

Emotional healing

Emotional healing includes such things as overcoming fears, adjusting to widowhood, or accepting the death of a loved one.

Relationships

Relationships can involve a close friendship or family tie or can show a relationship that overcomes an obstacle and is healed. This can also be the acceptance of a person with the only change being in the mind of the writer or main character.

Distant past

Childhood and young adult experiences can also provide good stories. Hindsight often presents wisdom, not readily seen while going through an experience, that can be passed on to others.

Adventure

By using the danger and suspense of true life experiences, you can grab the reader's attention.

Conversion experience

By sharing how someone became a Christian, others can be led to the Lord.

Personality profile

People enjoy reading about the lives of others, especially if their names are known or they have been through an interesting experience.

Organization or group

Often groups have an interesting history or ministry that the reader may not be aware of.

Whether writing about yourself or others, be careful not to come across as sounding too perfect. Show your flaws as well as the positive points. Paint a realistic picture when writing about other people too. Only then can your reader identify.

Before you polish your personal experience story, decide what your market will be and write to that market. Read all the magazines you consider potential markets, studying them in detail to become familiar with them. I'd suggest reading several issues of a periodical before submitting a manuscript to it. See Chapter 25 for marketing tips.

Tips for
Great Interviews

To imagine yourself inside another person...is what a story writer does in every piece of work; it is his first step, and his last too, I suppose.

—Eudora Welty

Many people don't have the ability to tell their own stories. That is where we, as writers, enter the scene. We can write another person's story for him through an interview.

I've written four books from interviews as well as many articles and stories for magazines and church school take-home papers. There are a number of publications that buy personal experience stories written by people other than the author.

When you look for people to interview, I don't recommend searching for famous people like Max Lucado or Chuck

Swindoll. They probably won't have time to meet with you. Instead, look at the people around you; and find an interesting individual in your church. Perhaps a boy from your congregation, for example, won an event in the Special Olympics for those with handicapping conditions.

Also read the local interest column in your newspaper, and keep a file folder of potential people to interview. But a word of warning—don't interview too close to a tragedy. A person who has suffered a traumatic experience needs a little distance to obtain proper perspective. Be sensitive, and show empathy.

Another approach is to keep a file folder of interesting subjects for possible interviews. Once you find a subject, research it. Then find an expert in the field, and interview him. Research and interviewing go hand in hand. People love to speak about what interests them—hobbies, vocations, talents. And you can be the apprentice learning at the master's feet. For other suggestions regarding research, see Chapter 5.

Remember to do your homework before the actual interview takes place. If the person has written a book, read it. Learn all you can about that person before you interview him. You don't want to waste valuable time asking questions you can find answers to on your own.

Questions for an Interview

Here are some questions you might consider asking your subject:

1. Do you have any special words you live by?
2. Was there a time in your life when you felt closest to God?
3. Was there a time when you felt God was far away?
4. When did God dramatically answer prayer in your life?
5. When did you feel most challenged?

6. Is there an incident in your live that could benefit others?
7. Have you ever been afraid?
8. When was the most special time in your life?
9. Have you ever experienced failure?
10. What is the most vivid memory in your past?
11. What would you most like to be remembered for?
12. What would you still like to accomplish?

These questions are only guidelines; don't use all of them in one interview. Instead, pick the ones most suited to your interviewee; and add your own questions to the list.

Interviewing Tips

Here are twenty tips that will help you during the actual interview.

1. Call and make an appointment with the person you have chosen to interview. Always be businesslike.
2. Try to allow ninety minutes to two hours for the actual interview if possible. An hour may not be enough time to gather all the necessary information.
3. Be on time, and dress appropriately. A good rule of thumb is to dress one step above the person you are interviewing. Then you will look professional.
4. Put your subject at ease during the first five minutes. Smile and chat informally.
5. Turn on your tape recorder. You want to get the words right, particularly if you are going to quote the person. Also you want to write in the interviewee's style. Listen for favorite words, mannerisms, and accents. Use the educational level and culture of the person, but don't use the exact words. You can't write exactly like the person speaks. You must edit, edit, edit—whittle away the excess. The

tape assures accuracy and helps you to get the intonations of the speaker's voice on paper when you do the write-up.

6. Assure the person the tape is confidential. Tell him you won't use sensitive material if he isn't comfortable with it, but that information often gives you background information vital to your understanding of who he is or why he did something.

7. Take notes as well as recording the conversation, but try to maintain eye contact at all times. You can probably type faster from notes than from cassettes, so notes are important. But your eye-to-eye contact is vital.

8. Be sensitive while interviewing as well as in writing the story afterwards. There is a tremendous amount of emotional tension during an interview. An individual feels vulnerable and naked once his feelings are down on paper.

9. Put new batteries in your tape recorder before going to the interview. Also check the sound to make sure it is working and is set at the correct level. The person can be intimidated if you spend a lot of time testing your tape recorder at the beginning of the interview. Buy an inexpensive lapel mike, and clip it to the interviewee to assure good sound.

10. Prepare a set of questions in advance. Arrange your questions in sequential order with the easiest to answer at the beginning. Save questions for the end that the interviewee might find threatening.

11. Be willing to deviate from the questions. If you ask, "When did you start collecting rare coins?" and she answers, "Right after I shot my mother-in-law," your next question isn't, "How many coins do you now own?"

12. Avoid questions with yes or no answers. You want as much of the story as possible to be in the interviewee's words, so keep the questions open-ended.

13. Try to visit the setting of your story. Doing so will help you paint the scene accurately as well as gain a flavor for the location.

14. If it is impossible to visit the scene, obtain detailed descriptions of it. Ask for pictures to borrow if possible.

15. Keep the person in line with your focus. People tend to ramble. If you allow this to happen, much of your valuable interview time will be wasted.

16. Be sensitive, and show empathy. Know when to probe and when to back off. Interviewing is an emotional experience, and a bond is formed between you and the person you are interviewing. So make yourself vulnerable. If the interviewee is self-conscious, tell him about a similar incident in your own life. Some people don't want bad things said about them, but our vulnerable areas help others the most. If he opens up, get permission to print what he says.

17. Keep your questions simple, asking one at a time. Prompt the person if she draws a blank.

18. If you become confused, stop and summarize what you think the person is trying to say. It is important your facts are accurate.

19. Be an exceptional listener. Most of the conversation on the tape should be the interviewee's voice, not yours. You won't learn any new information by listening to yourself.

20. Ask for a follow-up phone call in case you need it. This leaves the door open if something is unclear or you forgot to ask an important question. Leave your business card, and write a thank-you note.

Writing the Interview

Normally for an article, I recommend allowing the person to see the final draft you plan to send to the publisher. Don't let him make unnecessary changes, however.

Decide whether this article is going to be written in the first person or the third person. All *Guideposts'* articles are first person, but a number of magazines prefer third. Study your markets before writing.

First person has more depth. You can step into the individual's mind, heart, and eyes and tell it from his viewpoint. If you write personal experience stories from the first person viewpoint, then you have a decision to make. How important is it for your name to be on the byline? If your name does not appear, you are considered a ghostwriter.

Personally, I prefer to have my name on everything I write. I choose not to ghostwrite. I'm not saying that practice is wrong, but I feel it is misleading to the reader if the true author's name doesn't appear somewhere on the work. Credit should be given where credit is due.

In articles, the name of the person interviewed is placed first, then "as told to" and the writer's name. For example, "The Providential Escape" by Henry Fahman as told to Susan Titus Osborn. On leader's guides and other pay-for-hire work, the words "prepared by" often precede the author's name. On these kinds of projects, the author's name usually goes inside the book or booklet, rather than on the cover. For instance, Leader's Guide for *You Gotta Keep Dancin'* by Tim Hansel prepared by Susan Titus Osborn. On books, the actual author's name is placed second after the person whose story is being told. The names are separated by "with." For example, *You Start with One* by Deo Miller with Susan Titus Osborn.

Do the write-up while your memory is still fresh. The colder your notes get, the less you will be able to decipher them. Plus time will dull your enthusiasm for the interviewee and the subject matter.

During the interview, I take detailed notes. When I am ready to do the write-up, I transcribe my notes on the computer.

Then I listen to the tapes and add anything necessary that I didn't get down on paper. I stop the tape frequently, double checking my words for accuracy and clarity.

The next step is to edit, edit, edit. Trim the dialogue. Write and rewrite. Remember, the person wouldn't need you if he could write his own story. You will have lots of material you won't use; ultimately, you may even have enough for two articles. I had twenty-six tapes from Deo Miller in my basket of oysters, and I was searching for the pearls that would make interesting stories for the book.

Another nice thing about writing from interviews is it eliminates writer's block. It's not just you and a blank piece of paper when you sit down to write. It's you, a mound of notes, and a cassette.

The realm of manuscripts that can be written from interviews is unlimited. In 1990, I went to Hong Kong, Sri Lanka, India, and the Philippines to obtain information for my books written from interviews. But don't forget that your best story may be in your own backyard, in your church, in your local newspaper, or in your head.

Chapter Fourteen

Devotionals to Remember for a Lifetime

A drop of ink may make a million think.

—Lord Byron

The best devotional takes five minutes to read, yet it can be remembered for a lifetime. One reason I like to write devotionals is the feedback I receive from people across the country and around the world.

You want people to be influenced by what you write. You want them to say, "That's what I needed today." Or "I didn't know anyone else felt that way." It's amazing how you can touch people's hearts in so few words with a devotional.

If God hasn't touched your heart on a particular subject, you aren't going to reach your reader. Write from your experiences. Write about what is around you—the everyday occurrences. Be aware of interesting details or parallels in life. Write from your heart.

Devotionals may be the shortest items you will write. They are normally only 250 words long, although some range up to 400 words. They must be concise and to the point; there is no room for unnecessary words here.

If devotionals are well written, they can help a variety of people who have different concerns and needs. Each individual will draw something different from the same meditation. You achieve universal appeal by keeping your examples general enough so a number of people can identify with them. Also, the same devotional may strike one individual in totally different ways at various times in his life, depending on the circumstances at a given moment. So try hard to make your devotionals deep and broad based.

Often the audience for devotionals is phenomenal. Mary Lou Redding, managing editor of *The Upper Room*, says their devotional guide is read or listened to by eight to ten million people. It is the most widely read devotional guide in print.

Besides reaching many people, devotionals are an excellent way to break into print. A publishing house may not want to take a chance on a first-time author with a book because the risk involves thousands of dollars if the first print run doesn't sell out. But Mary Lou Redding says they would like to use 365 different authors in *The Upper Room* each year, and many are first-time writers. You can obtain their writer's guidelines from their Web site at www.upperroom.org.

Other daily devotional markets are listed in Sally Stuart's *Christian Writers' Market Guide* under the topical heading of devotional. Many of these are written on assignment only, but don't let that stop you from submitting. If you write quality devotionals or get some published, you can send them as samples and ask for an assignment on speculation, meaning the editor is not obligated to buy them if you don't deliver what he or she is looking for.

Components of a Devotional

A devotional normally has three components although you should check the guidelines for whatever market you wish to submit to because they do vary.

Bible Verse

The first component is a Bible verse around which the devotional is created. Be careful not to tack one on at the end. And don't write the devotional and then try to find a verse to submit with it. Instead, start with your Bible verse. Creating the devotional with a scriptural base will add depth to it.

Personal Experience

The second component is a personal experience. It can be yours or another person's. Devotionals can be written in first or third person; it doesn't matter usually. The important thing is to have a good anecdotal experience. Then bring in a spiritual application that ties the personal experience to the Bible verse.

Prayer

The third component is a prayer at the end, which is usually short, compact, and the crux of what you are saying.

Characteristics of Good Devotionals

Mary Lou Redding suggests eight characteristics of good devotional writing, which are used here with her permission.

Scriptural Base

Good devotional writing is Scripture based. It is grounded firmly in Bible study. It grows out of meditation and reflection on the Holy Word and its meaning for our lives. Don't take words out of context or use Scripture inappropriately, however.

A Fair Trade

Good devotional writing is a fair trade. It offers your insight in exchange for the reader's time and effort in reading the meditation. Use this principle regarding every piece of writing you do. The reader should never feel cheated at the end of reading a meditation, a filler, an article, or a book. Provide something new and unusual.

Appropriate Style

Good devotional writing has a style that is appropriate to the content or purpose for writing. When you teach, your communication should be direct, with clear use of speech. Don't make the reader struggle with your words. Also, you can't get too much emotion in 250 words, so don't try to deal with issues that are too heavy for the length of your piece.

Concreteness

Good devotional writing is concrete. It deals with what you have seen, touched, and heard rather than abstract concepts. Consider the images Jesus used to help people understand Him. He used bread, water, sheep—everyday items that people living in biblical times as well as today could understand.

Economy

Good devotional writing is economical. You want to deliver your message in as few words as possible. Be concise. Don't attempt to impress people. Just direct them to God's truth.

Strong Images

Good devotional writing is full of images. It produces strong images in the reader's mind. I would much rather read a good book than see a movie because my imagination is more vivid than the Hollywood portrayal. Perhaps many readers feel the same way.

Authenticity

Good devotional writing is authentic. It is not affected or preachy. Don't use Christianese—Christian clichés that only certain denominations use. You want non-believers to grow from your words, so they need to understand what you are saying.

Good devotional writing is a real person writing to other real people about what it means to live faithfully in a particular situation. It is the author saying, "This is how God is real for me." Authentic meditations acknowledge that life is complex and sometimes difficult, while pointing to hope in God.

Exploration

Good devotional writing is exploratory. It is not arrogant or preachy. It invites people to explore with you God's truth. It doesn't offer final answers. It says, "This is my experience. Is it the same for you, or is it different?" You invite the reader to make connections by providing images that will link his or her daily life with God's ongoing activities in the world.

Writing a devotional is a good exercise in fine-tuning your writing. You have only 250 words to focus one idea. In this small amount of space, you need to make your piece real, establish reader identification, and offer a tentative application for how the reader might act on your point in his or her life.

Writing for Children

I try to write on my knees under the authority of God and at eye level with the child, never at the child.

—Christine Harder Tangvald

The world population has more than doubled from 1950 to now. Three babies are born each second. From the age of three up, there are at least sixty million boys and girls; and each one is a potential reader of what you write.

More than 5,000 children's books are printed each year by 160 publishers, making 45,000 children's books currently available. Children's magazines have a combined circulation of more than 35 million copies. Children's books comprise the fastest growing market in both Christian and secular publishing. Children's books usually have a longer shelf life than their adult counterparts, and Christian books have a longer shelf life than their secular counterparts—making this an excellent market for which to write.

Many people want to write for children because they don't like the way young people behave. This is a mistake. You must love children to be able to write for them.

Writing for Children

Before I describe different types of children's markets, let me give you some general tips on writing for children of all ages.

Girls will read about boys, but boys don't like to read about girls. You can double your audience if the main character is a boy.

Use as few words as possible. Write concisely in all your work, but particularly for this audience. Write concretely, with step-by-step instructions or events. Make sure the concept you are dealing with is on a child's level, not an adult's. Children don't start thinking abstractly until they reach junior high school.

You need to be totally in tune with the age level you are writing for. Know their likes and dislikes and use their language. Most of the time, you need to use words kids are familiar with. Occasionally you can teach a new word, but be sure to define it in context.

If you have children or grandchildren, have them read what you write and critique it. If you don't have children in your family the same age you want to write for, find some kids in your neighborhood, teach church school, or sponsor a youth group.

Take-home Papers and Magazines

If you are unpublished, I do not recommend starting with books. Instead, one of the largest markets for new authors is church school take-home papers. I began my writing career twenty-one years ago by writing for these. Both denominational and nondenominational houses publish take-home papers for children of all ages. They come out weekly, offering many opportunities to sell your stories, articles, and fillers. Also you can continue to sell your material as reprints once it has been published the first time. See Chapter 24 for more information on rights.

There are many subjects you can sell to the take-home paper market. Fiction, particularly for 4th- to 6th-graders and young teens, is popular. The length is normally about 1,000 words. How-to articles, nature and domestic animal stories, and paraphrased Bible stories are often included in children's take-home papers. These nonfiction articles are shorter, about 500-800 words. Check your writers' market for the correct length for the particular publication you have in mind. Also crafts, puzzles, and activities find a market here.

Many adult periodicals print children's stories as well as children's magazines. Most children's markets do not require a query letter because the manuscripts are so short, but check your writers' market.

Curriculum

Once you become successful at selling to take-home papers and/or magazines, you might consider moving into curriculum. Curriculum is usually done on assignment, but publishers often use freelancers to do the writing. Although the opportunities are limited because curriculum is not often updated, it is interesting to write a quarter's worth of material or a few lesson plans, depending on how the publisher operates. Teaching at the age level you are writing for is required for this type of writing. You might want to start with your own denomination if it publishes curriculum.

Now, let's look at the writing opportunities in books.

Picture Books

The main market for preschoolers is picture books, most told in story form with beautiful color illustrations. The purpose of these books is for the parent to read them to the child. So keep in mind that you are selling to the parent. You have two to three seconds to hook mom or dad. In the first paragraph, readers need to meet the main character who is doing something interesting; and every page must contain action.

SPREADS FOR A 24-PAGE PICTURE BOOK

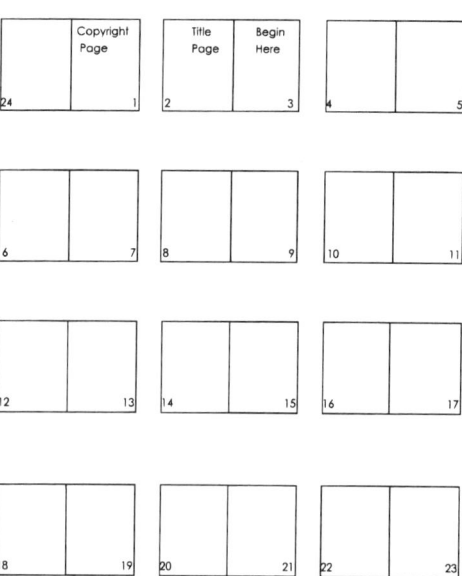

Picture books have a definite format, and you must know this format to write them. It can be difficult to form a mental image in your head, but think of the entire book starting out as an enormous sheet of paper, cut up in multiples of eight. Board books are 16 pages with 14 pages of text. Picture books are 24 (20 pages of text) or 32 pages (26-28 pages of text). Over half of the picture books are in a 32-page format.

Text and pictures are laid out in spreads. A spread is two pages that spread across the book when it is open. Sometimes there is text on one side of the spread and a picture on the other; sometimes there is text and pictures on both sides. If page 1 is the copyright page and page 2 is the title page, then page 3 is where the text begins. Pages 4 and 5 would then make up the first full spread. Spreads have equal pieces of writing on them. If you have 26 pages of text, you will have 13 or 14 spreads.

Picture books contain lots of color, humor, and a clear message. They need to make a point, to teach a lesson. The greatest benefit for the child is that Mom gives her undivided attention while they read the book together.

Easy Readers

Another type of book you might consider writing for children is the easy reader with a simple vocabulary for the child to read by himself. It must be concrete since young children do not think abstractly. Each sentence contains a subject, verb, and an object. The words should flow in a rhythm with six to nine lines on a page. These books are usually forty-eight pages with a word count of 1,000-1,400 words. They contain pictures, but not as much room or money is invested in the artwork as in picture books.

First Chapter Books

These books are the first books kids read that actually have chapters. Plus the entire book is about the length of the first chapter of an adult novel. These books usually contain some pictures, often black and white.

Beginning readers are proud of the fact that they can finally read, and first chapter books are the bridge for them from picture books and early readers to juvenile novels. First chapter books have eight to ten chapters and are 6,000 to 8,000 words long. The difficulty comes in developing well-defined characters and a complete story in such a short space. Dialogue is crucial to the success of a first chapter book.

Young readers enjoy humor and mystery thrown in with their action, and I recommend a single viewpoint character to prevent confusion and promote reader identification. First person works well but is not necessary.

Juvenile Novels

The hottest market in all of Christian writing currently is juvenile fiction for eight- to twelve-year-olds. These fourth through sixth grade books have large type. They normally contain about 20,000 words with no pictures.

These are fast-moving books with lots of exciting action. The dialogue must be believable and true to that age group, and they contain strong character development. Normally a publishing house will want a series of these, so you need to think in multiple books if you want to write them. Occasionally, you might be able to fit your book into an already existing series.

Another market is the junior high group. The print in these books is smaller, and the word count increases to around 30,000 words.

All the qualities that make good adult fiction also make good junior fiction: conflict, suspense, pacing, focused plot, complex characters, a strong beginning, a tense middle, and a satisfying ending.

How do we write materials for kids that they will want to read—books and stories that will teach them to question, to analyze, and to think for themselves? We do so by writing stories.

Children seldom show interest in nonfiction books, particularly those dealing with issues or instructions on how to lead their lives. Fiction is the best way to capture their attention because young people are not threatened by pretend stories.

They think books are an escape from the problems around them into a world of fantasy. They read to be entertained.

But actually you can meet these young readers' real needs by addressing their felt needs. We can help young readers identify with our characters to solve their own problems. We can't tell them though; we must show them. They will read and see for themselves.

Our young people need to affirm their own experiences. They need to know that others have survived the everyday problems they are struggling with. Some need to learn not to take themselves so seriously. Others need to learn to be more accountable.

Through our writing, we can show them there is hope and love in the world. We can show them biblical principles. Perhaps we can help them establish their own personal relationships with Jesus Christ or strengthen their faith by the words we write. May this be our goal in writing for children.

Chapter Sixteen

Spellbinding Short Stories

Tell a good story. And let it bring your characters to a different place (in soul and/or body) than where they started out.

—Catherine Breslin

Currently one of the fastest growing markets in all of Christian writing is fiction. However, if you are a beginning writer, I do not suggest you start with a novel. Instead, write a short story for a church school take-home paper.

Lee Roddy offers an excellent definition of fiction: "Creating characters in conflict, culminating in crisis and change with commentary." The four key words are character, conflict, crisis, and change, called the Four Cs of Fiction. The tips I give in this chapter will work for fictional techniques in nonfiction pieces as well as for fiction stories.

Create a Story

Write to the needs of your audience, not your own needs. The acrostic OPNAD, another Lee Roddy creation, may help you remember this fact: Other People's Needs And Desires. Needs include those of the publishing house as well as the reader, so match what you are writing to a specific market. Know what publishing houses are looking for and what length manuscripts they want. Find out who their audience is. Go to writers' conferences and talk with editors.

Write what you know; write from your own experiences, changing details as needed. You don't have to undergo the exact experience you are writing about, but it is vital that you feel passionately about your subject. If you are writing about your life, though, make sure others will benefit from what you have to share. Even a short story has to answer the question, "So what?" It needs to have a point that will provide take-away value for the reader—something he can take into his own life to benefit him.

A story is comprised of three elements: theme, plot, and character.

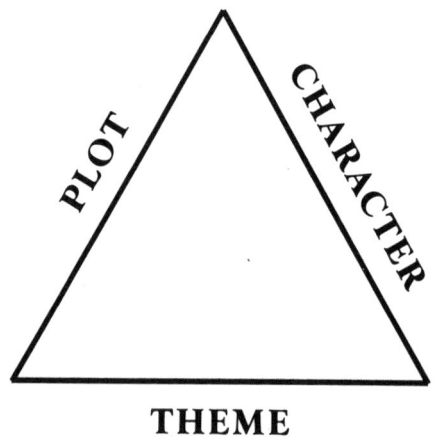

THEME

Normally you can think of theme as the foundation on which the story sits. Your focus sentence will be based on the theme or main point you are trying to achieve. The story is either character driven or plot driven, depending on whether the main character is the most important element or whether the story line is more important. These three qualities are always integral parts of your story, regardless of your emphasis.

As in other writing, compose a focus sentence and an outline. Also plan how you will end the story. This may change as the story unfolds, but you need to know where you are going. You may prefer to write a synopsis, a brief summary of the plot, rather than an actual outline. The shape you will use to structure your story is the shape of a prism mentioned in Chapter 10.

Once you have the structure established, write your first rough draft. Don't try to edit as you go along. Instead, allow the words to flow. After you write the story, allow some time to pass before you start rewriting it.

In the first paragraph, you must hook the reader. Open with the viewpoint character and an exciting beginning that makes him want to read on. Write your story as seen from one person's viewpoint, either first or third person; third person is usually easier to write. Paint a brief picture of your main character, showing his or her personality, so the reader can see him and identify with him.

For example, here's an opening from *The Hair-Pulling Bear Dog* by Lee Roddy (Colorado Springs, CO: Chariot Victor, 1996, p. 11):

At first, D.J. Dillon thought the terrible nightmare had returned. In his sleep, he again heard the squeal of brakes, the crash, and then the awful silence. The 13-year-old boy's blue eyes blinked open. He stared into the soft moonlit darkness of the kitchen where he slept on a rollaway bed.

His blond head turned automatically toward his parents' bedroom wall beside him. He started to call softly, "Mom?" Then he remembered.

Develop Characters

Your characters need to appear authentic, whether they are real people or not. They must be real to you, or they will never seem genuine to your readers. So take time to develop these individuals in your mind. Then write a character sketch of your main character as well as the secondary characters.

Here are ten tips that will help you create character sketches:

1. Is your character male or female? Why?
2. How old is your character? Why not younger? Why not older?
3. Give a physical description of your character. What does his or her physical description tell you about the theme or conflict?
4. Describe your character's emotions and personality.
5. What does your character believe about himself, the world around him, God, and life?
6. What problem does your character face? How did this problem arise?
7. How does your character think this problem can be solved? Why won't this proposed solution work?
8. What does your character need to learn, experience, or believe before the problem can be resolved?
9. What experiences (conflicts) could bring your character to this insight or change?
10. Will your reader grow or change? Why or why not?

You won't use all the information in your character sketch in your story, but you must have a picture of the person formed in your mind. To explore a character's feelings in depth, mentally step into his skin and write from his viewpoint. In this way, your characters will assist you in writing your story. They can help you bring it alive in ways you couldn't by yourself.

Paint a Scene

Develop a location for your story that readers can picture in their minds. Use all of your senses so the reader can live the experience with you and feel like he or she is there. If you are painting a beach scene, for example, hear the thunder of the waves crashing on the shore. Taste the salt from the spray. Smell the clean, crisp air. Feel the soft breeze brushing across your face.

The following example is from the opening of Chapter 1 of my book, *Eyes Beyond the Horizon*:

> Not a leaf of the flame trees stirred on Marpi Cliff. Douglas Campbell found the stillness foreboding and unnerving. In the early morning dawn he watched the dark clouds as they formed a circle around the tiny island of Saipan. The menacing clouds hung back on the horizon, brooding, threatening with an evil intent to sweep land and sea into their possession (p. 15).

Narrative is used here to tell a mini-story from the narrator's viewpoint. It also sets the scene, so the reader can sense the approach of the typhoon and feel its momentum building.

As you write short stories, take readers on a journey with you and captivate them with your spellbinding story.

Chapter Seventeen

Creating Characters in Conflict

Times are bad. Children no longer obey their parents, and everyone is writing a book.

—Cicero

Without a problem to solve or a conflict to overcome in a story, the reader quickly becomes bored. Therefore, you need to introduce the problem as close to the beginning of the story as possible.

Introduce a Problem and Set the Mood

Set a mood that matches the nature of the situation. The reader wants to feel a part of the events as they unfold. Never hold out on your reader; he will feel cheated. He should know as much as the main character does during the development of the story.

The example below, taken from the opening of Chapter 9 of *Eyes Beyond the Horizon* sets an ominous mood by using such phrases as "inky pools of tree shade," "torch darting in the blackness," and "stabs of summer lightning." The reader knows something dangerous is about to happen.

> A bright moon, sweeping across the starry midnight sky, washed over the transmitter buildings of Christian Radio City Manila with a dim white light. It picked out the figure of a guard as he passed between inky pools of tree shade, his torch darting in the blackness like stabs of summer lightning....
>
> In the stillness, night sounds carried across the heavy atmosphere with astounding clarity. The footsteps of an announcer crackled on the gravel as he walked along the roadway between the quieted compound houses....
>
> Behind the night-hushed scene stood a tall antenna tower, pinnacle by red warning lights. At the top, a man held by his head dangled helplessly three hundred feet from the ground! (p. 115).

Establish Conflict

Conflict is essential to your story. In fact, without conflict you have no story. There are three types of conflict: person vs. person, person vs. self, person vs. environment or God.

Go to your library or local Christian bookstore, read lots of story openings, and take notes. See how authors introduce conflict. Then decide how you would resolve the conflict if you were writing the book. This is an excellent exercise to improve your fiction skills.

When you are writing a short story, limit your characters to two to four with only one in conflict. In a book, you can keep introducing complications upon complications, solving some as you go along and waiting until the end to solve the main conflict.

Build suspense, being careful not to reveal too much. Surprise the reader, and provide an interesting twist. Don't allow him or her to figure out the ending before you get there.

Be careful not to allow the characters to take over. You must know what they are going to do. That is why you write the ending—or at least a brief summary of what will happen—after you write the beginning. Don't manipulate the characters into implausible actions or conflict. They must be believable, or you will lose credibility with your reader.

The main character must solve his own problem. He should get a just reward, whether good or bad; but in the Christian market, you usually find a happy ending. Don't leave the ending up to the reader or leave any loose ends. The reader should have a sense of completion and feel comfortable after finishing your story. A "problem solution story" is much more powerful than a "come to realize" ending.

Help the reader to identify with the main character to solve his or her own problems. You can't tell him though, you must *show* him. If you preach at your reader, you will lose him. Include lots of dialogue, using words that are simple and relevant today.

Stories need to be filled with action. Stay out of your character's mind, and keep the story focused on his activities. Once in a while, you can tell what he thinks but not often.

After you reach the climax in your story, be brief and be gone. Wrap it up as quickly as possible, being careful not to leave any loose ends. Once you reach the climax, the reader won't have any reason to keep reading.

Set your story aside for a week, then go back and rewrite and rewrite more. Ask yourself, "Will it hurt the story if I leave out this word, this paragraph, this entire scene?" If not, take it out. Whittle away all the dead wood. Make sure your characters are well developed and the main character solves his problem, averts disaster, or overcomes his opponent *himself*. Your scenes should move along smoothly and transition well from one to another.

It doesn't matter if you are writing fiction or nonfiction, using the fiction techniques in this chapter and the last one will strengthen your manuscripts. People love stories. They want to escape from real life into an imaginary adventure, but they need help with their problems too. You can meet their real needs by meeting their felt needs through the vehicle of fiction. And God can teach spiritual truths through your fictional characters.

Chapter Eighteen

Keys to Successful Fictional Techniques

A good writer is basically a storyteller, not a scholar or a redeemer of mankind.

—Isaac Bashevis Singer

Whether you are writing fiction or nonfiction, a basic understanding of the use of fictional techniques will bring your writing to life.

Narrative and Exposition

Narrative is the objective reporting of your story, that which can be pictured visually in concrete images in the reader's imagination. It is what the characters do in the action of the story. Exposition is information, often interpretive and/or subjective, funneled through the viewpoint character to shed light on the action. It includes comments, opinions, reactions, explanations, and feelings. (These are novelist Carole Gift Page's definitions, used with permission.)

Faulty exposition interrupts the narrative flow, shatters the illusion of reality, and embarrassingly reveals the mechanics of fiction writing (just like a playwright jumping on stage and interrupting a play during a performance). Instead, good writers weave exposition subtly into the action so it doesn't interrupt the narrative flow. Proper exposition appears to derive directly from the viewpoint character's thoughts or memories.

Three-D Technique

In the proper blending of narrative and exposition, the author communicates information to the reader through (1) what the characters say, (2) what the characters do, (3) what the main character thinks, and (4) what the main character remembers. This blending is achieved by using detail, dialogue, and description, the components of the Three-D Technique.

Detail

Use the specific rather than the general.

Dialogue

Direct conversations between characters, especially characters in conflict, reveals their personalities. Dialogue moves the story along and turns narrative into interesting conversation. Set your characters apart by developing a different speech style for each one.

Description

Draw from all five senses to describe the setting and characters. Use sight, sound, smell, taste, and touch to create a mood.

Notice how the Three-D Technique is achieved in the following script.

The Case of the Missing Jade
Episode 2

Establish setting	Jonathan rushed through the crowd
Time and place—Narrative	toward the Taipei police station. He
Description to create a	held his first Associated Press assign-
mood	ment in his hand, and he could not
Exposition	wait to tell Yen-chi. He paused for a
Introduction of main	moment in the doorway before run-
character	ning up the steps to his cousin's sec-
	ond floor office.
Introduction of minor	Yen-chi glanced up at the excited
character	reporter. "What's that?" he asked.
Dialogue—Mini-scene to	"My first assignment," Jonathan
impart information	replied. "I'm going to Singapore to
regarding main	cover the International Flower Show
character	at the Botanical Gardens. Not a page-
	turning assignment, but there should
	be some dignitaries there. Maybe I can
	find a hidden story."
Suggested foreshadowing	"Maybe, indeed," replied Yen-chi,
	chewing on the end of his pencil.
Character trait	"Plus, I may be used as an inter-
Detail funneled through	preter since I speak English, Taiwanese,
dialogue	and Mandarin."
Personality development	Yen-chi didn't comment. He was
through dialogue	lost in his own thoughts. "Aren't you a
	citizen of both the Republic of China
	and the USA?" When Jonathan nod-
	ded, Yen-chi continued, "That can
	help you cross cultural boundaries—
	should be helpful."

Introduction of second
minor character

Description

Detail funneled through
minor character's
dialogue

Background information

Dialogue

Nature of long-range
conflict indicated

Detail

Mini-scene ends

Transition

Telescoping narrative, com-
pressing time and action

Jonathan looked at Yen-chi. "Why do I get the feeling your mind is not on what I'm saying?"

"Quite the opposite, my cousin," replied Yen-chi. "Did you ever meet Shu-ying Huang?"

"No, I don't think so."

"Well, you are in for a treat," said Yen-chi with a sly smile. "Our families have been friends for generations. Her parents moved to Singapore about ten years ago and opened a jewelry store. After Shu-ying completed her education in Taipei, she joined her father as his office manager. Shu-ying is my contact whenever I need information from Singapore."

"Sounds like I'm going to Singapore on two assignments."

"Actually, I'm happy Singapore is your first assignment. Some of the missing jewelry has turned up in the Huangs' store. I don't want the thieves to know we found it—at least not yet. I want you to find whoever sold it to the Huangs. Contact Shu-ying when you reach Singapore. Here's her number."

Jonathan left the following morning for Singapore and arrived late afternoon at the Huangs....

Her long straight hair was tied back fashionably with a yellow bow,

Description of minor character	accenting her high cheekbones. Jonathan realized he was going to enjoy more than the flower show in Singapore.
Exposition	"Hi, you must be Jonathan Chen," she said, moving around the counter to greet him.
Dialogue	Jonathan stepped forward, and she reached out her hand. "And you
Narrative—Character development through dialogue	must be Shu-ying. Yen-chi described you perfectly." He noticed she was not wearing a wedding ring, and his heart beat faster.
Foreshadowing— Transition	They talked for a while about mutual friends in Taipei. Then Shu-ying said, "Let me get those papers I photocopied for Yen-chi. If you come
Dialogue	into the back room with me, I'll show you the stolen jade."
Elaboration of problem	The jewelry set consisted of a jade necklace, bracelet, and earrings. The necklace featured large, irregular chunks of deeply polished jade held
Detail	together with hand-formed, 24-carat
Description	gold. The bracelet and earrings matched. It was the most magnificent set of jewelry Jonathan had ever seen.
Dialogue	"Here's the name and Hong Kong
Detail	address of the person who sold it to us. He called himself Howard Wong. I thought his name might be an alias, so I wrote a description of him."
	Jonathan glanced at the paper:
Exposition	Howard Wong. It was a common

127

name. He would check out the address when he got to Hong Kong.

As he read Shu-ying's description of Howard, he developed an uneasy feeling that the assignment he was doing for his cousin might be dangerous. He would have to be careful whom he trusted. But for now, he needed to hurry over to the Botanical Gardens. The flower show would soon begin.

Exposition
Foreshadowing

Sets the mood for the next episode—Reader wants to keep reading

Bring your writing to life by using fiction techniques in your nonfiction as well as your fiction. Blend narrative and exposition, using detail, dialogue, and description.

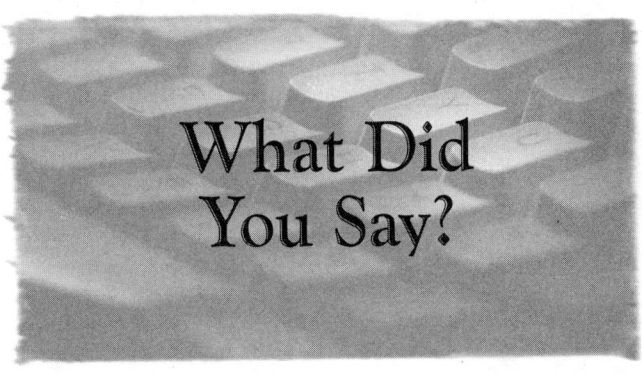

Chapter Nineteen

What Did You Say?

Speak your dialogue out loud. If it sounds like the way people talk, then write it down.

—Tom Clancy

Good dialogue moves the action of a story along. Dialogue can be used effectively in fictional stories, personal experience stories, devotionals, and anecdotes within articles and nonfiction books. Here are some tips for using authentic dialogue in your manuscripts.

Multiple Characters

When possible, have at least two people in your story or scene, so they can talk to each other. If this is not possible and only one person is involved in a happening, perhaps you can relay that incident after it occurs through a telephone conversation or a chat over coffee. Staying in someone's mind and listening to his thoughts is a boring place for the reader to be.

Conversational Speech

Dialogue should be kept simple, natural, and conversational. However, don't use the exact words a person would actually speak because, in normal conversation, a person uses far more words than is needed. Actual speech needs to be whittled down, so it is crisp and clear. Never let your characters ramble.

Once you have a detailed character sketch of your main person, you will know how he will react in certain instances. You will be aware of his feelings, ideas, and beliefs. Consequently, his personality will come out in his speech. He will help you write the dialogue because, if you know him, you will know what he will say.

As your reader gets to know your main character, he knows what the character will say too. If your main person acts out of character, the reader will know and feel something is wrong.

Also be careful not to contrive your character's speech or have him preach. The reader doesn't want to be talked down to—either by you or the main character. We teach readers lessons by what the main character learns, not by lecturing.

Tags

Be careful of the tags you use for dialogue. "He said" is better than "he articulated" or "he uttered." After all, what is important is the information between the quotation marks, not the word used for "said." An exception would be if you need to show strong emotion or a certain voice tone that the words by themselves don't express. For example: "He shouted"; "he whispered."

A word of warning: You can't smile, sigh, or laugh words. Instead of writing, "You're cute," he smiled, use "You're cute," he said with a boyish grin.

Punctuation

Commas and periods always go inside the quotation marks. Question marks and exclamation points go inside if they are part of the dialogue and outside if they are part of the entire sentence. For instance: Why did I keep hearing over and over in my head the words, "I'll never forget you"? Before he said good-bye, he asked, "Will I ever forget you?"

Example

Here is an example of a devotional that is almost entirely dialogue, taken from my book, *Rest Stops for Single Mothers*. Notice how the dialogue moves the story along and maintains reader interest.

The Fire

Faith can place a candle in the darkest night.
—*Author Unknown*

"Mom, I had to abandon my car," my son's voice sounded breathless on the other end of the telephone line. "Flames were jumping across the highway. Burning branches fell into the back of my convertible."

"Are you OK?" I asked, concern filling my voice.

"Oh, Mom, I'm fine, but I'm worried about my car."

"Tell me what happened. Maybe I can help," I offered.

"I was on my way home from class, and I could see the fire burning out of control in the Santa Barbara hills, but it seemed far away. The freeway was blocked, so I took the old highway towards town. About halfway there, people on either side of the road had been told to evacuate their homes. Everyone was trying to leave. There was a huge traffic jam. Suddenly, flames jumped across the highway, and that's when it happened."

Rich was talking so fast that I didn't understand everything. "That's when what happened?" I asked.

"My clutch cable snapped, and I couldn't shift gears. I pulled over to the side as far as I could and had to abandon my car."

"What did you do then?"

"I called my girlfriend to come and get me. Mom, I can't afford to lose my car. I don't have comprehensive insurance on it, and I'll have to drop out for a semester if I can't get to school."

I knew Rich was right. Rich's finances for his college education were extremely tight. Without his car, he'd have to leave school and obtain a full-time job to earn money for a new one. I saw no alternative.

"Let's pray about it, Rich. God knows the situation."

I rarely pray for material possessions, and I've never prayed for a car before, but this time I did. "Lord, You know Rich needs that beat-up Volvo convertible to get to his college classes. Please spare it in this fire. We pray that the fire will soon be contained."

Three days later, I received another call from Rich. "Mom, they finally let me check on my car. I caught a ride back to where I left it. The fire burned to within a hundred feet, and it's full of ashes; but it runs. It's in the shop now, getting a new clutch cable."

God has taught us to pray specifically. In this case, He knew how important that car was to Rich's education. He spared the car, and I learned an important lesson. When things look bleak, when money is tight, God is there, showing His presence in the smallest details of our lives (pp. 103-104).

Whenever possible, introduce dialogue into your writing. It will help to move the story along in an interesting manner for the reader.

Chapter Twenty

Getting the Editor's Attention

You never get a second opportunity to make a good first impression.

—Mark Twain

Editors reject many excellent articles for various reasons. Perhaps your article starts in the third paragraph, and you were just getting your thoughts together in the first three. Or if the editor requested a query letter, and you sent the entire manuscript, he may not even read it because he knows you didn't study the publishing house's guidelines. If you sent a query but didn't explain clearly what your article is about, you probably won't get a chance to do so later. Remember—your most important job is to get the editor's attention.

What Editors Are Looking For

One of the main questions you have may is: Exactly what is an editor looking for? Following are five things editors have told me they look for in articles and stories.

Sharp Focus

An article should stay on target. In the first chapter, we talked about developing a good focus sentence. Make sure your theme is developed throughout the piece and you don't stray from your focus. If your article rambles or deviates on a tangent, it will be rejected.

Clean Copy

An article should contain no errors. Magazine editors are extremely busy and are always working on tight deadlines. They don't have time to rewrite your manuscripts. Make sure you have crafted each article as smoothly as you are capable of and you have checked the grammar, punctuation, and word usage for errors.

Appropriateness

An article should be appropriate to the readership of the magazine. Study the demographics of each magazine and take-home paper you are considering sending your manuscript to, so you can get to know the audience. If you are writing an article on time management, for instance, your slant for parents of young children will be different than your slant for teens. Editors say the number one reason they reject manuscripts is that the subject matter is inappropriate for their publication.

Pizzazz

An article should have pizzazz. Write about subjects you feel passionately about, and your emotions will come through in your writing. You must care about your subject for your reader to get enthused. You need to hold the reader's attention for the article to be worthy of publication.

Reader Involvement

Editors want to print articles that directly impact their readers. When a person finishes reading your article, will it move him to action or make him want to change his life in some way? Try to find a way to make the reader play an active role in your article.

Why Editors Reject Manuscripts

Let's take a moment to talk about rejection. When you start sending your manuscripts to editors, you can expect rejection. The more you submit, the more rejection slips you probably will collect.

At writers' conferences, often a free book is given to the person who has received the most rejection slips the past year. Strangely enough, this person often gets the award for the most articles and stories sold too. Rejection and acceptance go hand in hand.

You can't expect to sell every article you submit, nor can you count on always selling it to the first publishing house you send it to. However, if a manuscript is repeatedly rejected, you should check it over closely to see if it is well focused. Perhaps it needs to be rewritten.

Another reason for rejection is sending the piece to an inappropriate market. Studying your markets carefully can help solve this problem. Or perhaps that publishing house recently printed a similar article. There are many reasons for rejection that have nothing to do with the quality of your article.

Also remember that the editor who rejects your manuscript is rejecting something you wrote—not you personally. Not all rejections are final. Editors change jobs often. If your manuscript is well-written and targeted to a certain market, resubmit it a year later, and the next editor might publish it.

Before you mail your manuscript, make a list of other publishing houses that could be potential markets. You can create a spreadsheet in a computer program like Excel to use for this purpose. Then if the article is rejected, immediately send it to the second house on your list. Your articles and stories don't benefit anyone sitting in your drawer.

Selling Editors with Query Letters

The first impression an editor has of you, the writer, is the manuscript you submit and/or your query letter. A query letter is a letter of inquiry asking if a publication would like to see a completed article on a specific subject. Make your query letter professional, to the point, and short. Keep it one page in length if possible.

You can create your own letterhead stationary on a computer by using special fonts and a laser printer. If you don't have these, ask a friend who does to print a master copy of your stationary for you. Then you can photocopy it at a nominal price. You can also inexpensively make your own business cards. Blank stationary and business cards are available at most office supply stores and through mail-order catalogs.

A query letter should answer four questions:

1. Why are you qualified to write the article?
2. What is the article about?
3. Who is your audience?
4. Why will this article interest the reader?

See the sample query letter on the opposite page.

You can determine whether a publication wants to receive a query or the entire manuscript by checking Sally Stuart's

Susie Writer
1 Longhand Lane
Beach City CA 90000
310- 555-1212

June 1, 2000

Mr. Jerry Joyful, Acquisitions Editor
Slickcover Magazine
1000 Everprint Street
Anytown IL 60000

Dear Mr. Joyful:

In July, I attended the American Christian Writers' Conference where I met your assistant editor, Bill E. Buyer. He suggested I query you with my idea for a 1,500-word article, which I feel will fit your guidelines.

For the past five years, I have volunteered in a home for unwed mothers. One sixteen-year-old named Sara has given me permission to write her story under a pseudonym. I feel the choices she made will help other young girls make the right decisions regarding sex and marriage.

Sara became pregnant and considered abortion. Since she is only sixteen and a junior in high school, she did not feel she could adequately care for herself and a baby. A strange turn of events led to a harrowing experience that resulted in Sara's decision to have her baby and give him up for adoption.

The primary audience is young teenage girls—particularly those considering sex outside of marriage. The secondary audience is pregnant teens. Also mothers and friends of girls going through the trauma of an unwanted pregnancy will benefit from this article.

This article is timely because today seven out of ten teenage girls are sexually active, and three out of ten will eventually become pregnant out of wedlock. Let me know if you would be willing to see my article, "Sara's Song," on speculation. I look forward to your response.

Yours in Him,
Susie Writer

Christian Writers' Market Guide. If a periodical wants your entire manuscript, still include a cover letter that contains the same points as a good query so the editor can use it for quick reference.

If you write a quality query letter, there is a good chance an editor will ask for your entire manuscript. When he does, write "requested material" on the outside of your mailing envelope. Always include an SASE or a postcard so the editor can let you know if he is interested in your article or not.

Fiction pieces, poetry, shorts and fillers, and most children's stories usually do not require a query letter. Many magazine markets, however, will require one. Remember, you are not in the publishing house to personally talk to the editor, so your letter serves as your introduction. Make it the best you can.

Chapter Twenty-one

Putting on the Polish

We are all apprentices in a craft where no one ever becomes a master.

—Ernest Hemingway

Once you have rewritten your article or story and it is as good as you are capable of getting it, then it's time for someone else to look at your work. Here are seven questions writers often ask about polishing their manuscripts.

What is a manuscript critique?

Webster's College Dictionary defines a critique as "1. an article or essay evaluating a literary or other work; review. 2. a criticism or a critical problem on some subject, problem, etc." As a verb, it states, "3. To review or analyze critically."

As Christian writers we use the term critique as an evaluation of a manuscript, weighing the good and bad points, in an attempt to make it publishable.

Can you objectively critique your own work?

Because we are emotionally involved in our own manuscripts, we cannot objectively evaluate them well. We should edit each project to the best of our abilities, however, before finding someone else to look at it. Doing so may involve many rewrites.

How many times should I rewrite a manuscript?

There is no answer to this question; writing is not an exact science. It actually depends on what you are writing, how well your manuscript is coming together, and how long the piece is.

Christine Tangvald, author of numerous children's picture books, says she rewrites her picture books an average of thirty-five times. Most novelists do not rewrite their entire books that many times, but they may rewrite the opening scene numerous times. Many authors say they rewrite their manuscripts a minimum of five times.

It has been my experience that beginnings and endings are the most difficult parts to write, whether I am writing a devotional, a short story, an article, or a book. The middles may require far less revision.

Where can I find others to look at my work?

Before seeking professional help for your manuscript, you should find other writers, friends, and/or neighbors to evaluate it. Make sure you look for people who will give you an honest critique, not just say, "That was simply wonderful." Almost every rough draft needs to be reworked.

Also it helps to have people who will comprise your target audience read your material, even if they aren't writers. For example, if you are writing a young teen novel, find several junior highers to read your proposal to see if it holds their attention.

Ideally, for a line-by-line critique, you should join or form a local critique group with two to four other writers. Meet together monthly (or whatever fits in your schedules), and evaluate each other's work. You will learn a great deal about the craft of writing by critiquing other individuals' manuscripts.

Personally I think it is best to read the manuscripts silently at a critiquing session and write comments directly on them. I'd also recommend that each person write his or her suggestions in a different color ink, so the person being critiqued can easily tell who made which comments. The group may have difficulty objectively evaluating manuscripts if each person reads his work aloud. Some people are better readers than others. Plus reading a number of articles aloud is time consuming.

At the end of the session, the group can discuss each manuscript. Be sure to make positive as well as constructive comments to each person, and be willing to *listen* to the constructive criticism of your own material.

After the session is over, consider carefully the comments made as you rewrite your manuscript. Take it back to the following meeting and have it critiqued once again. Keep up this process until your critique group thinks your manuscript is ready for submission.

Sally Stuart's *Christian Writers' Market Guide* contains a section on writers' clubs. I suggest you contact one in your area to see of they have a critique group you can join.

Should I seek the services of a professional critique service?

Once your manuscript is as good as you can get it, you may desire to seek a professional critique service, such as the one I direct. One of the fourteen editors of the Christian Communicator Manuscript Critique Service can evaluate your work, recommend changes, and suggest markets.

An in-depth critique, like the one we provide, offers line-by-line editing for grammar, punctuation, and word usage, as well as an overall content evaluation. In the overall evaluation, the critiquer looks at the structure of the story, article, or book proposal. She makes sure the manuscript is theologically sound; has a strong beginning and ending; has good transitions; and is presented in a logical, sequential order.

If the manuscript is well focused, she will also suggest potential markets. Approximately thirty publishing houses suggest our services, and a critique from one of our editors will provide an avenue for a closer inspection by the acquisitions editor of a publishing house.

Won't an agent or an editor critique my work for me?

Because of the volume of manuscripts handled by most publishing houses, editors usually won't consider a manuscript unless it is close to publishable. If a magazine editor chooses to publish an article or story, though, a certain amount of content editing will be done before it is printed.

Also the entire periodical will be copyedited for spelling and punctuation errors. The author, however, doesn't usually see the final form until he or she receives a complimentary copy of the magazine or take-home paper. Book editors also follow a similar procedure, but a book author sees the changes before the book goes to press.

Agents will rarely give a line-by-line critique on a manuscript. They make their money by taking a percentage of royalties on a book once it is published and selling. An agent rarely takes money up front except for postage, telephone, and other such expenses. Beware of agents who ask for an up-front fee!

Agents are not necessary in the Christian publishing industry, and most will not accept authors unless they are producing two to three books a year. Agents rarely accept clients for articles and stories.

Would I benefit from attending a writers' conference?

The investment of your time and money in attending a writers' conference is invaluable. Writing is a lonely business, and it can encourage you to meet with other writers who share the same thoughts and goals. Conferences provide an excellent opportunity for you to improve your writing, editing, and marketing skills. They are also wonderful places to meet editors, find out what types of articles and stories they are looking for, and sell what you have written. Plan to attend a writers' conference in your area, or use your vacation time to attend one in another part of the country. Check the *Christian Writers' Market Guide* for a complete listing of Christian writers' conferences.

If there isn't a conference nearby, consider taking a writing course by mail or e-mail. My Christian Communicator Hands-on Class is available on cassette and by e-mail. The *Christian Writers' Market Guide* has a section of writers' resources like these.

Good writers are constantly reading new information, learning new skills, and developing new ideas. An author never reaches a point where he or she has learned all there is to know about the craft of writing. That is what makes this field so exciting.

Submitting Your Manuscript

The successful editor is one who is constantly finding new writers, nurturing their talents, and publishing them with critical and financial success.

—A. Scott Berg

When you are ready to type your article in final form and send it to a publisher, use the format below.

Mechanics

Double space your manuscript on white, twenty-pound bond paper with one- to one-and-a-half-inch margins all around. It is permissible to use computer or photocopying paper, but send a clean copy. Use twelve point Times New Roman,

Courier, or Courier New font, and leave the right margin unjustified (ragged). Usually the preset, standard margins in a computer word processing program are acceptable as is the default font. Put a heading on each page, and number each page.

Format

Here are some items that go on the first page:

Susan Titus Osborn
3133 Puente Street
Fullerton CA 92835
714-990-1532
Susanosb@aol.com

First rights
About 1200 words
©1999 Susan Osborn
SS# 521-00-0000

The Fire

by Susan Titus Osborn
or
by Susan Lee Taylor
(a pseudonym)

"Mom, I had to abandon my car." My son sounded breathless and desperate at the other end of the telephone line. "Flames were jumping across the highway. Burning branches fell into the backseat of my convertible."
"Are you OK?" I asked.

Left Heading

Always put your name, address, telephone number, and e-mail address in the top left corner of the first page of the manuscript. If an editor needs to contact you, she has your phone number and e-mail at her fingertips.

Right Heading

To maintain balance, these are the four items that can be placed in the top right corner of the first page.

Rights

On the first line, list what rights you are offering. Normally, if this is the first time you are selling your article or story, you will offer first rights, giving an editor one-time rights to publish your material before you offer it to another publication. Sometimes these rights are called First North American Rights which includes the United States and Canada or First North American Serial Rights if it is a serial publication. Do *not* offer your article or story elsewhere until after it comes out in print the first time if you sold first rights.

Once your article or story has been printed by the publication to which you first sold it, then you may sell second or reprint rights. Copies of this same manuscript can be sent simultaneously to different publications, but make sure they don't have overlapping audiences. For instance, you wouldn't want to send it to two Southern Baptist publications at the same time.

Word Count

On the second line, write the approximate number of words. If your article or story is over 500 words, round off to the nearest hundred. If you've written a filler under 500 words, estimate the count to the nearest 50 words. Normally, you can figure 10 words to a line, 250 words to a page. Four pages equal approximately 1,000 words.

Copyright

The third line is for your copyright information with the copyright symbol, year, and your legal name.

Social Security Number

Your Social Security number goes on the fourth line. A publisher cannot pay you unless the accounting department has your Social Security number. Your check may be delayed if an editor has to ask you for it at a later date. At the end of the year, you will receive 1099 income tax forms stating your earnings from different publishing houses. The Internal Revenue Service requires a 1099 form if your income was over $600 from any given publisher.

Title and Byline

Skip down a few lines, and center your title. This space leaves room for the editor to make notes on your manuscript during the production stage.

Under the title, center your name the way you want it to appear on the article. If you are using a pseudonym, this is where you place that information. I suggest placing the words *a pseudonym* underneath, so there will be no confusion at the publishing house when making out your check.

There are several occasions when you might feel it's beneficial to write under a pseudonym. They are:

1. If you are writing about sensitive material and you want to protect yourself or other family members, use fictitious names for everyone.
2. If you are a woman and you want to write for men, you might consider using a male pseudonym or vice versa.
3. If you are prolific and a magazine or take-home paper is going to have more than one article by you in an issue, the editor may want you to write the second one under a pseudonym.
4. If you are co-authoring but just want to use one name, you could develop a pseudonym that includes parts of both of your names.

Subsequent Pages

Use a header with your last name and a key word from the title in the top left hand corner of the second and all subsequent pages. Put the page number in the top right corner of all but the first page. For example:

Fire - Osborn   Page 2

Mailing

Before mailing your manuscript, make a second hard (paper) copy and back up your computer copy on a disk or tape. Computers can crash and take all your information with them. Never mail the only copy of your article or story, and never fold a manuscript. Place it in a 9 x 12" manila envelope. Include another folded 9 x 12", self-addressed, stamped envelope (SASE) if you want your manuscript returned; or include a self-addressed, stamped postcard if you don't want it back. Mail your manuscript to a specific editor, not just a publishing house. If you've met an editor at a conference, it helps to mention that person by name in your cover or query letter. Remember to look in a market guide to see if that publication wants a query letter or the entire manuscript. For more information on marketing, see Chapter 25.

To increase your sales, target appropriate markets for your manuscript, make it look as professional as possible, then submit your article or story to a publishing house.

Keeping the Paperwork Straight

Writing is putting one's obsessions in order.

—Jean Grenier

People often tell me, "I don't consider my writing a business. I just write for fun." However, if you are spending time and money trying to get your manuscripts published, you can legally claim those expenses on your income tax return. Plus, if you keep the paperwork straight from the beginning, it will save you a lot of time later. And if your chair is comfortable and your screen and keyboard are the right height, your neck and back won't be so inclined to interfere with your craft. So even if writing is an avocation for you, consider it a business.

The Business Side of Writing

Whether writing is a vocation or an avocation for you, treat it as a profession.

Office

Ideally, you should have a desk and filing cabinet dedicated solely to your writing—an entire room is even better. Many writers, however, do not have this luxury. The important thing is to be able to keep your paperwork straight, so you will be able to find things when you need them.

Also it is important to have a comfortable chair that adequately supports your back. Writing requires a lot of sitting. Be sure to get up and walk around at least once every hour. The better shape you keep your body in, the sharper your mind will be for creating and editing.

Even if you don't have an actual office location for your writing, you can still get the job done if you keep things in order. If you don't have a metal filing cabinet, you can purchase an inexpensive cardboard one at an office supply store. I suggest you buy a box of file folders and label them. If you are like me, you would rather write than organize files, but lack of organization can cost you precious hours of trying to locate information on an article you wrote several months or years ago.

Label one file for each project you are currently working on. Once an article is finished, continue to keep a file folder for it. Keep your research notes in it as well as tear sheets of publishing credits. Any research you have done for an article should be labeled in a manner that will help you find it quickly should you decide to write a second article on the same subject at a later date.

Also set up files for ideas that pop into your mind, ones you don't have time to develop yet. Whenever you find an article or story on a subject you intend to write on someday, place it in a file folder under that category.

Stationery

Another item I feel is important for a professional image is letterhead stationery. Subconsciously, editors are more impressed if your cover or query letter is typed on your own letterhead. There are a number of paper companies, as well as office supply stores, that sell four-color stationery. If you don't want the expense of this type of paper, type your own letterhead on twenty-pound bond paper. You can add graphics if you desire. If you have an ink jet or laser printer, you can reproduce your own stationery. If you don't have a quality printer, take your letterhead on a disk to a photocopying store for reproduction. Make sure you use a quality copier to reproduce it though.

Business cards are another item you will need. These are convenient to hand out at writers' conferences to editors and other writers with whom you want to keep in touch. These, too, can be created and printed on a laser printer. Again, you can use four-color cards or plain white, depending on your budget.

Computer

If you haven't invested in a computer yet, I strongly suggest you do so. Used Pentiums, 486s and 386s can be purchased inexpensively. Plus there are many discount computer companies that sell new systems at a reasonable cost. IBM dominates the computer industry, so be sure to buy a computer that is IBM compatible.

For software, I recommend Windows and Microsoft Office. The word processing program I use is Microsoft Word. Always back up your work on disks or a tape as well as printing out a hard (paper) copy. I've had three hard disks fail over the years.

Also buy a laser printer if you can afford one or an ink jet printer. After all, you only look as professional as your manuscript does. The editor can't see *you*.

Many periodical editors are requesting articles and stories on disk or by e-mail. Most book publishers will insist on receiving your book manuscript on a disk, or they will charge you a fee if they have to key it in since book publishing is done almost exclusively electronically today. Most publishers, however, do not want submissions by fax.

Tax Tips

Following are some tax tips I have learned through the years. However, I am not a tax expert, so please check with a tax preparer (enrolled agent, registered/licensed tax preparer, or CPA), the IRS, and/or your state tax agency if you have any questions.

If you are actively writing and seeking publication, you are a professional freelance writer and have a business that entitles you to deduct expenses. Many of you may think the work involved isn't worth bothering with, especially if you didn't show a profit—but it is! A certain period of time, usually three years, is allowed for a beginning business to start showing taxable profits. You may think of your writing as a hobby or avocation, but if you are trying to market your product, then you *are* in business. Claim your expenses and lower your income tax!

Income Statements

When a publishing house pays in excess of $600 to an individual within a year's time, it is required to report it on a Form 1099 to you and the IRS. These forms reflect income you've earned during the year and must be included on your tax return just like a W-2 Wage and Earnings Statement from a job.

Deductible Expenses

Let me reemphasize that even if you did not make a profit, you can still fill out Schedule C, claiming your expenses for the year. Save your rejection letters; they are excellent proof of your intent and efforts to earn money as a writer.

Keep a ledger and save your receipts. Quicken and Excel are good computer programs for tracking your income and expenses.

Some of the deductible expenses you need to keep track of are stamps, business cards, stationery supplies, computer supplies, publications, books on writing, telephone calls to editors and for interviews, writers' conferences, and dues to writing organizations. They add up quickly. You can also deduct travel costs for business purposes, as well as a percentage of your meals and entertainment if they are directly related to your freelance writing.

There are expenses related to having an office in your home that are also deductible, including a percentage of your utilities, maintenance and upkeep, and even depreciation. You must have a designated room as an office that is not used for *anything* else to take these deductions. Deducting a portion of your home for depreciation can be tricky though. A word of warning: Watch the laws concerning the sale of your home. Deducting an office can affect your capital gains. When you sell your home, any depreciation taken in prior years has to be claimed as income and can impact the tax line.

Deductions do add up. Personally, I have written off six computers, two college degrees, and an assortment of other expenses. The computers have all been used for my business, not for family computer games. Both of my degrees (a B.A. in Religious Studies and an M.A. in Communications) were considered job-related. When I go on vacation, I often incorporate business into my trip, so I can write off part of the vacation. However, I only write off the percentage that directly relates to my freelance writing.

If your writing expenses add up to more than your gross sales, you can claim a loss and deduct it from your declarable income—lowering your taxable income. Be careful! IRS rules state that you must show a profit after the third year. If you are audited and you failed to show a profit by the third year, the IRS can declare the whole business a hobby. The hobby tax rules are different from the business ones, and you could find yourself owing taxes on back years for expenses claimed that are not allowed because they exceed your income (i.e., no losses are allowed for a hobby). You need to be able to prove you are running a business and attempting to make a profit. Check with your tax preparer.

Self-employment Taxes

If your net business income is $400 or more within one year, you must file Form SE for your self-employment taxes. The IRS free publications on how to file these forms are excellent. The one I have found most helpful is Publication 334, *Tax Guide for Small Businesses*. Call your local IRS office to obtain forms and pamphlets, or contact them on their Web site at www.irs.ustreas.gov.

Remember! If you are actively writing and seeking publication, you are a businessperson. Be sure to run your business accordingly with accurate records and receipts to back up your deducted expenses. Again, check with a tax preparer (enrolled agent, registered/licensed tax preparer, or CPA), the IRS, and/or your state tax agency if you have any questions.

Treating your writing as a business, taking expenses you are entitled to, and cutting down on your declarable income leaves more money to donate to church and mission organizations. Thus, one ministry can serve another.

Understanding Rights and Copyright Law

Writing is the only profession where no one considers you ridiculous if you earn no money.

—Jules Renard

M any people confuse the term *copyright* with the term *rights*. This chapter explains the difference between all rights, first rights, and reprint rights as well as providing a basic understanding of copyright law. You will also learn when you can quote another's work without his or her permission and when doing so is plagiarism.

Rights

Rights are different than copyright. When you sell first rights to a publication, you are offering one-time rights to publish your material before you send it to another publication. Sometimes these are called First North American Rights, which includes the United States and Canada, or First North American Serial Rights if it is a serial publication.

Once your manuscript is printed by the publication to which you sold first rights, you may then sell reprint rights, sometimes called second rights. When you sell reprint rights, your duplicate manuscripts may be sent out simultaneously to many different publications. Try to avoid selling to two publications with overlapping audiences, however, such as two periodicals or take-home papers published by the same company or denomination.

When you sell first rights, you still own the rights to that work. After the publication date, the rights revert back to you. Selling reprint rights doesn't affect your rights in any way.

One-time rights give a publisher the opportunity to print your material one time. Personally, I never use this terminology because it is confusing as to whether your material has been published previously or not.

If you sell all rights to your manuscript, then the publisher owns your work; and you cannot print it elsewhere without getting written permission from that publishing house. Try not to sell all rights if possible. Work-for-hire contracts fit in this category. You normally receive a flat fee for these, and the publisher retains all rights and the copyright.

Usually you will be paid more for first rights than reprint or one-time rights, and often editors will be more interested in the piece. You will probably earn a third to a half as much for reprint rights. However, reprint rights are an excellent way to earn extra money by selling your manuscripts over and over.

Electronic Rights

With the increasing importance of electronic publishing, the matter of electronic rights has become an issue. Some book contracts include a clause for electronic rights (e-rights), while other publishers say that e-rights are covered by the section on subsidiary rights. But what about articles and stories? Usually contracts are not involved when selling these.

With more and more magazines developing their own Web sites and CD-ROMs, e-rights have become an enormous issue without clear-cut guidelines. If a person sells first rights, should a publisher be able to reprint that article on a Web site without the author's permission and without additional compensation? Unfortunately, the meaning and scope of e-rights has not been precisely defined; and, as a result, courts have differed on their interpretation of the law. I think if a person sells first rights, the publisher should be required to pay the author a reprint fee if his or her article is used electronically.

Copyright Law

A copyright is a way to protect something you create, whether writing, painting, or drawing. A copyright gives you four specific rights: to copy the work, to take excerpts to use elsewhere, to sell selected rights to the work and make money from it, and to perform or display the work.

What can you copyright? Anything that is your original work—articles, poems, stories, pictures, songs, grocery lists. Anything you write down can be copyrighted except ideas, concepts, facts, news, and titles. Anything regarding the expression of ideas can be copyrighted.

Since the laws were changed in 1978, you do not have to register your work with the Copyright Office to hold a copyright on it. Once your original material comes off your printer, typewriter, or pen, you own the copyright on it. If someone plagiarizes your work, however, and you want to sue him for copyright infringement, then you need to register your article, story, or book with the Copyright Office in Washington, D.C.

Most magazines are copyrighted, and their copyright doubly protects your personal copyright. Newspapers are seldom copyrighted, although syndicated columns are protected. Government publications are not copyrighted either. If you author a book, the publisher will register your copyright; but make sure he registers it in your name, not the name of the publishing house.

If you wish to copyright your material as a safeguard, send a copy of the manuscript, a registration form, and $30 to: Publications Section, LM-455, Copyright Office, Library of Congress, 101 Independence Avenue, SE, Washington, D.C 20559. The telephone number is 202-707-3000. The hot line number to request forms is 202-707-9100. Or you can download forms on the Internet at www.loc.gov/copyright. You can register as many of your articles, stories, and poems as you like under the same copyright, as long as all the material is sent to the Copyright Office at the same time.

The copyright registration is effective on the date of the receipt in the Copyright Office. For material written after January 1, 1978, your copyright lasts for seventy years after your death. For manuscripts you wrote before that date, your copyright is for twenty-eight years plus a renewal for forty-seven more for a total of seventy-five years.

Once a copyright expires, the work goes into public domain. The public may use it at no cost at that point as long as the copyright isn't picked up and reregistered by your heirs. Also, public domain only applies to the original work. If material is revised or updated, it may not be in public domain. So be sure to check your sources.

If you need information or guidance on legal matters, such as disputes over the ownership of a copyright or suits against possible infringers, you may need to consult an attorney.

Fair Use

Fair use is defined as the right to use copyrighted work without permission or without making payment to the owner. Copyright law provides for the fair use of another's work without infringing on his copyright. How much can you copy from a source and stay within fair use?

The law is designed to be vague. If you are copying a magazine article, you can probably copy a paragraph or two. Also you can probably copy several paragraphs from a book without infringing on copyright. Be careful, though, not to copy the essence of something. Poems and songs can only be copied without paying a high fee if they are in public domain. If a song is currently popular, use only the title. Titles are not copyrightable, but if a book is in print, you cannot title a new one by that name.

Always give the author you are quoting credit for his material, even if you are within fair use and aren't required to obtain his permission to use it. Cite your source in a footnote, end note, or within the text of your article or book.

If you are going beyond fair use and you want to quote from copyrighted material, be sure to obtain permission from the copyright holder. You do this by writing the author or the publishing house. Look in the author's biography or on the copyright page for information in contacting him. If the author wants payment for quoting him, you are usually the one who pays rather than the publisher. I always try to stay within fair use when quoting sources to avoid extra expenses.

Trademarks

Capitalize trademarks (i.e., Xerox, Kleenex) to avoid problems in this area. You can also put a trademark symbol after registered trademarks, such as Happy Meal™.

Plagiarism

Plagiarism is copying, using, or closely imitating someone else's material without permission. Be careful that you don't plagiarize. This is easy to do unintentionally, especially if you don't take accurate research notes.

In closing this chapter, I'd like to quote my dear friend and colleague, Jack Cavanaugh who often quotes Wilson Mizner: "When you steal from one author, it's plagiarism; if you steal from many, it's research."

Chapter Twenty-five

Finding the Right Markets

We are called to write, and I feel we will be held responsible at the Judgment for the people who are hurting that we could have helped, but didn't, because we didn't write what God laid on our hearts to write.

—Harold Ivan Smith

To write well and sell what you write, you need to be informed. Read all the books and magazines you have time for. I think it is necessary to read as many hours as you write. You have to pour in, or there is no fountain of information from which to pour out.

Attend writers' conferences and pick up all the free publications and guidelines you can. Subscribe to magazines such as *The Christian Communicator*, *The Writer*, or *Writer's Digest*.

Writer's Digest Books has a series of secular books on writing, and ACW Press has a series of Christian books on writing, such as *A Complete Guide to Writing for Publication* (Susan Titus Osborn, ed., 1999). *The Complete Guide to Christian Writing and Speaking* (Susan Titus Osborn, ed., Orange, CA: Promise Publishing, 1994) is another excellent resource. All these books are available at Christian writers' conferences or from my office.

Identify Potential Markets

Sally Stuart's *Christian Writers' Market Guide* (Harold Shaw) is your number one tool for marketing. Purchase and study her annual guide carefully. Then decide which publications you would like to write for, and send them each a postcard. Ask for a sample copy of their magazine or take-home paper and their writers' guidelines. Most take-home papers and some magazines also have theme lists. Be sure to ask specifically for these if applicable. If you are on the Internet, you can obtain writers' guidelines from many publishing houses online. Check the *Christian Writers' Market Guide* for online addresses.

Study the Markets

Once you receive these materials, place them in file folders in your file cabinet to study and use as resources. You need to be familiar with a publication, as well as comfortable with its style and basic views, to write for it. Read your magazines carefully, and study them thoroughly.

Do a market analysis of each one. See what articles are similar to the type you have written. Analyze each article in detail. If you are looking at a nonfiction article, see how many anecdotes it uses. Then check the number of statistics, quotations from experts in the field, case studies, or other information that gives the article credibility beyond the author's personal opinion.

Try to determine the demographics of the readership. Do this by studying the advertisements, the letters to the editor, and the slants of the articles. The closer you can tailor your article to what the editor is looking for, the better chance you will have of selling that article.

The length of your article or story is determined by the publication you are writing for. Again, check your writers' market. A good rule of thumb is about 1,600 words for articles and 1,200 words for stories.

Beginning writers often ask: "Should I write my article and then find a market, or should I find a market and then write my article?" Let me answer that question, referring back to my three-step writing method in Chapter 1. I suggest you form a focus sentence, develop an outline, and write a first rough draft. Then study the markets to see where your article might fit before you polish it and put on the finishing touches. That way you won't waste many hours writing something for which there is no market.

Once you have determined appropriate markets for your article or story, make a list of them in the order you want to send out the manuscript. You can also use this list to keep track of postage spent for your bookkeeping records. Then mail your article to the first publishing house on your list, complete with an SASE or postcard for the editor to mail a reply back to you. Be sure to send it to a specific editor. (See Chapter 22 for more submission tips.)

Marketing is as much a part of the writing process as putting the words down on paper and editing them. Be sure to allow enough time to study the markets carefully and to submit only to appropriate markets. In the long run, this work will save you both time and money.

Conclusion

As you begin your writing career, remember that God is in charge. Some of you will publish books someday, but beforehand you will need to serve your apprenticeship. Others will write articles and stories. Many are called to write, but few are chosen to be professional writers.

Some of you may be called to write for church newsletters or may find a ministry of writing personal letters to friends, relatives, or missionaries. These, too, often change lives. A few of you may find that writing isn't what God had in mind for you after all. And that's OK, too. God has given each of us special talents. He expects us to use these talents to glorify His name.

In closing this book, I'd like to share with you a piece I wrote about Matthew. I have used this for speeches and have sold it a number of times with various revisions.

God's Call of Matthew

> "As Jesus went on from there, he saw a man named Matthew sitting at the tax collector's booth. 'Follow me,' he told him, and Matthew got up and followed him" (Matthew 9:9, NIV).

This is a familiar story to all of you, but let's look below the surface and see how a decision made in a split second changed a life.

William Barclay refers to Matthew as "the man whom all men hated." There was never a more unlikely candidate for the office of Apostle than Matthew. Let's look at this man by starting with his vocation as tax collector.

In biblical Palestine, a tax was levied on everything grown in the ground, on income, and on all goods and commodities as they entered and left the territory of Herod. The Roman government auctioned the right to collect taxes to the highest bidder. The man who bought that right was responsible to the Roman government for an agreed sum. Anything he charged above that amount was his commission. People had no tax charts, so they never knew what should be paid in taxes. This system led to grave abuses. Many a tax collector became wealthy through illegal extortion.

The hatred of the Jews for the tax collectors was violent, fueled by their religious conviction that God alone was King. To pay taxes to any mortal ruler was an infringement of God's rights. Tax collectors were prohibited from the synagogue.

Matthew was in his tax collector's booth when Jesus called him. Maybe he'd seen Jesus before. Perhaps he wondered if it wasn't too late to leave his old life and shame behind and start again.

At any rate, when Jesus called him, Matthew stood up and followed, leaving everything without a moment's hesitation. His decision, made in a split second, changed his life.

However, he paid a unique price for answering this call. The other disciples, who were fishermen, could return to their nets; but for Matthew to leave his post meant no turning back. Once he left the tax office, he could never return to this lucrative business.

I said he left everything behind when he followed Jesus. But he took one thing with him—his pen, or more precisely, his skill at writing and keeping records. Ultimately, he used that talent to compose the most quoted Gospel in Christian literature. Here is a shining example of how Jesus can use whatever gift a person may bring to him.

I'm sure Matthew found himself poorer in material things when he gave up his lucrative business. If you choose a full-time profession of Christian writing, you, too, may find yourself with less income than you could earn in a secular position.

But let's talk for a moment about God's promises and how Matthew benefited there. Although Matthew sacrificed much in the material sense, in the spiritual sense, he became an heir to a fortune. Matthew lost a comfortable job, but he found his destiny. He gave up a good income, but he ultimately found honor. Mark and Luke refer to him as Levi, but he called himself Matthew. Matthew means gift of Yahweh.

It may be that if you accept the challenge of Christ—whatever that may be for you—you, too, can become a gift of God. Perhaps you'll find a peace and joy in life that you never knew before. I know I have.

Jesus' calling of Matthew is one of the greatest instances of Jesus' capability to see not what an individual was but what he could become through Christ's power working within him.

There was nothing secretive about Matthew's decision to follow Christ. He openly invited his friends to his spacious home for a dinner with Jesus. The Pharisees called these friends sinners, meaning they were Jews who ignored or broke the Mosaic Law in either moral or ceremonial aspects. The Pharisees prided themselves in their righteousness. They felt no need for Jesus. They felt self-sufficient.

Matthew knew he needed Jesus. He wanted to be part of God's promises. Matthew's concern for his former colleagues is shown during this dinner at his home where Jesus was the guest of honor. No doubt Matthew's purpose was to win these men to Christ. He knew they needed Jesus too.

I challenge you to use your skills, as Matthew did, to glorify God. Allow God to pour His love into you. Then your love, your joy, your words can flow through your pen and touch others, allowing them to see a glimpse of Christ within you.

Your pen is permanent. Many of the stories, articles, and books you write will be here long after you are gone. Your words can influence people, persuade them to change their lives, and help them gain understanding as Matthew's words have done.

God uses ordinary people to do extraordinary things. He will use us if we will listen to Him and then go out and give 150 percent of ourselves to what He has asked us to do. If He has called you to write, you will find that writing is hard work; but it is rewarding.

Perhaps God is calling you now. Maybe a story you write will help a person struggling with a problem. Perhaps an article will bring a teenager to Christ. Wouldn't you like to arrive in heaven one day and have someone tap you on the shoulder and say, "You don't know me; but because of something you wrote, I'm here too"?

Works Cited

Osborn, Susan Titus. "The Case of the Missing Jade."
    Episode 2, *Studio Classroom*, March 1997. Taipei,
    Taiwan: Overseas Radio and TV.

Osborn, Susan Titus. *Potpourri of Praise*. Mukilteo, WA:
    WinePress, 1995.

Osborn, Susan Titus. *Rest Stops for Single Mothers*. Nashville,
    TN: Broadman & Holman, 1995.

Titus, Susan F. *Eyes Beyond the Horizon*. Nashville, TN:
    Thomas Nelson, 1991.

Titus, Susan F. *You Start with One*. Nashville, TN: Thomas
    Nelson, 1990.

About the Author

Susan Titus Osborn is a contributing editor for *The Christian Communicator* and director of the Christian Communicator Manuscript Critique Service. Susan is also an adjunct professor at Hope International University in Fullerton, California. She has authored twenty-one books and numerous articles, devotionals, and curriculum materials and is a publisher's representative for Broadman & Holman Publishers. She has taught at over 120 writers' conferences across the United States and in five foreign countries. She is listed in *Who's Who in America, Who's Who of American Women, Who's Who in the World, Who's Who in the West,* and *Who's Who in the Media and Communications.*

For a complete range of editorial services,
including contract advice, critiquing,
correspondence courses, and more
contact Susan at:
3133 Puente Street
Fullerton, California 92835

Phone: 714-990-1532
E-mail: Susanosb@aol.com
Web site: www.christiancommunicator.com.

Order Form

#	Title	Price	Total
	Just Write—Susan Osborn	$12.00	
	A Complete Guide to Writing for Publication—Susan Osborn	$15.00	
	How to Write and Sell a Christian Novel—Gilbert Morris	$12.00	
	Write His Answer—Marlene Bagnull	$12.00	
	An Introduction to Christian Writing—Ethel Herr	$17.00	
	SUB-TOTAL		
	+ S&H*		
	TOTAL		

*S&H: Add $4.00 shipping and handling for the first book and $1.00 for each additional book.

Purchase these books from your local bookstore or contact:

Write Now Publications
5501 N. 7th Ave, #502
Phoenix, AZ 85013

800-931-BOOK (2665)